Transform your parenting

"The only (emails) I read."

"I absolutely love your emails. I have to be honest,
they are the only ones I read from the MANY emails
I have somehow been subscribed to." –M.

"I needed to hear that."

"Thank you. I needed to hear that." –B.

"We've already seen a positive change."

"The tips are practical and implementable immediately.
We've already seen a positive change in our girls (4 and 2)." –M.P.

"Revelatory."

"This was so revelatory for me." –R.

**Get insights you can act on.
Join thousands who have signed up
for my free newsletter:**

www.zerotofive.net/sign-up

Pear Press
P.O. Box 70525
Seattle, WA 98127-0525
U.S.A.

This book may be purchased for educational, business, or sales promotional use. For information, please visit www.pearpress.com or www.zerotofive.net.

FIRST EDITION

Library of Congress Cataloging-in-Publication has been applied for

ISBN-13: 978-0-9989192-3-2

Designed by Nick Johnson/Cima Creative

Cover photo by Betty Udesen

Printed in U.S.A.

10 9 8 7 6 5 4 3 2 1

Pear
Press

ZERO
to
FIVE

70 Essential Parenting Tips
Based on Science
(and What I've Learned So Far)

TRACY CUTCHLOW

CONTENTS

Prepare

Peace and quiet, please (at first)	7
Bolster your friendships	8
Eating for two? Not exactly	10
Exercise thirty minutes a day	12
Sing or read to your belly	14
Stress less	16
Share the chores equally	18
If you're suffering, get help	22
Expect conflict as a couple	26
Know you can't truly be prepared	28
Envision baby all grown up	30

Love

Prepare to be amazed	34
Create a feeling of safety	36
Comfort newborn with the familiar	38
Cuddle with baby	40
Get in sync	42
Smile, hug, encourage	44
Include baby	45

Talk

Speak in a singsongy voice   50
Talk to your baby a ton   52
Read together   58
Say, "You worked so hard!"   62
Teach sign language   68
Plan playdates in a second language   71

Sleep, eat & potty

Guard your sleep   76
Guard baby's sleep, too   78
Help baby sleep better at night   80
Give baby chances to self-soothe   84
Crying it out, a certain way, is OK   88
Say "Excuse me" to keep kids in bed   92
Make bedtime less crazy   94
Be laid-back about breastfeeding   96
"Eat food. Not too much. Mostly plants."   98
Let baby decide how much to eat   102
Offer the opportunity to potty   104

Play

Let baby touch that	108
Save the box	109
Make music with baby	110
When kids snatch toys, wait and see	113
Play at self-control	116
What makes a great playroom	122
Make-believe	124
Nurture creativity	128
Ask "Why?" and "What if?"	130

Connect

Ask for help	134
Choose empathy first	136
Create more ups than downs	138
Know your child	140
Hold weekly family meetings	144
Put down your phone	146
(Almost) no TV before age 2	148
A little TV after age 2	150
Make screen time social	154
Encourage mistakes, discomfort, and boredom	156

Guide

Be firm but warm   160
Follow four rules about rules   166
Emotion first. Problem second.   170
Label intense emotions   172
Say what you see   176
Guide instead of punish   180
Plan ahead to avoid trouble   194
Rock your routines   197
Call a calm-down, not a time-out   199
Ask, "Can you think of a better way?"   202

Move

Rock, jiggle, and swing   206
Keep moving   208

Slow down

Be still   216
Don't bother to compare   220
Find your own work-family balance   222
Be more, do less   227

Could you use more calm and confidence?

Who couldn't? Most of us first-time parents have barely spent any time around babies before having our own. Everything is unfamiliar at best; terrifying at worst. My husband and I had our first baby in our mid-30s, after months of "should we or shouldn't we?" We'd spent about fifteen minutes around newborns before that point. Like many expecting couples, our only preparation consisted of birth-education classes. I spent untold hours researching diapers, clothing requirements, and gear. (As avid cyclists, we had a balance bike picked out as early as a baby swing.) These weren't much help in how to raise a baby. Unlike many expecting couples, I'd edited the childhood brain-development book *Brain Rules for Baby*. Very handy! But that was theory.

Reality is a shock. The sleep deprivation and utter uncertainty with a newborn. The joy of your toddler's exuberance. The heat rising in your face when he grabs a friend's toy and all eyes are on you. The love flooding your heart when your preschooler cradles your face in both hands and kisses you. The shock of betrayal when she hits you. The tantrums. The defiance. The exhaustion. The mess.

Parenting is an incredible experience, but it's the hardest thing any of us will ever do. We all need help to:

- get more sleep
- enjoy less stressful meals
- get our kids to listen to us
- tame temper tantrums
- calm our kids—and ourselves
- feel like we know what we're doing
- create a peaceful, happy home

We want to feel like we're enjoying parenting, not just surviving it.

And as baby surprises us, delights us, concerns us, bewilders us, and frustrates us beyond belief, we go looking for answers.

Maybe we ask friends. Mom. The Internet. But soon we're buried in opposing opinions ("Best thing I ever tried"; "Didn't work for me AT ALL"), vague parenting articles, and irrelevant forum comments.

I'll flip through the many brain-development and parenting books on my shelf. I pore through studies, staring at sentences like "Briefly, trajectory methodology uses all available developmental data points and assigns individuals to trajectories based on a posterior probability rule." All are filled with what seems, post-baby, like a very large amount of very small type.

And I think: it would be nice to have one inviting, just-tell-me-what-to-do, open-to-any-page collection of parenting's best practices, based on what the research says.

This is that book.

Where do I get off writing a parenting book? I'm not a neuroscientist or a child-development expert. Instead, I'm relying on those experts, and on my fifteen-year career as an award-winning journalist, to help me assess the scientific research and distill it into something readable for tired parents. I've sprinkled in anecdotes from my own life. Not because my experience is vast, and not because it will be exactly like yours, but to connect with you over the fun, weird, funny, tough moments that make up parenting.

I've focused on baby's first five years because they involve an incredible amount of change. When it comes to mobility, language, empathy, and motor skills, you can't tell the difference between a 30-year-old and a 31-year-old. But the difference between a 1-year-old and a 2-year-old? Remarkable. Amazing. Fascinating. Crazy. More than 90 percent of brain development takes place in those first five years.

So, these early years matter. We're setting baby up for success. And we're establishing our philosophies as parents, which will carry us well beyond five years. The themes in these pages—love, talk, play, connect, guide, move, slow down—are as important at 2 months old as they are at 2 years old, 5 years old, 15 years old, and even 50 years old. We're all human.

This book is rooted in research. (I don't provide a citation within the text for every study, just to keep a friendly flow, but you can find references in the back.) In trying to answer questions, researchers account for all kinds of variables, and they filter out bias as much as possible. Science is not infallible, but it's the best guide we've got. That and our intuition. Not only is every child different, but every parent is, too. All of these are reasons you may follow a piece of advice and get a different result, or not follow a piece of advice and get the same result. You just have to try things and see what works for *you* and *your* baby.

Parenting is a process of striving and repairing. Use this book as a guide, both to starting down a good path and to staying on the path you choose. Allow yourself mistakes and do-overs. Pause to pat yourself on the back when you feel proud. As much as you can, relax.

The truth is, what really matters in parenting are the big things: being responsive to baby's needs, truly being present when you're together, talking to baby a ton, being firm but warm in discipline, lots of hugs . . . and sleep.

We know what kind of parents we want to be. We want to raise pretty great kids and, despite all the challenges, do it with calm and confidence. This book is about how.

Best of luck to all of us.

Tracy

tracy@zerotofive.net
www.zerotofive.net

Prepare

Pregnant women tend to have a long to-do list. Put "weekly massages" on the list, and don't fret about the rest. Baby's needs are minimal: a couple key nutrients, whatever sleep and exercise you can manage, and low stress. Spend your time cultivating friendships.

Peace and quiet, please
(at first)

....

Can you turn your embryo into a genius in the womb?

No. For decades, product manufacturers have preyed on vulnerable parents-to-be: give birth to a smarter, calmer, more attentive baby who can already spell!

It started in 1979 with Prenatal University, a twice-daily program in which you pressed your pregnant belly while teaching your fetus words such as "pat," "shake," and "rub." Then came the Pregaphone, which amplified your voice into the womb so that you could communicate even earlier with baby. You placed a plastic funnel on your belly and spoke into a mouthpiece connected via a tube. Today's descendants include a belt that emits heartbeat sounds. You wrap it around your pregnant belly for two hours a day to train your fetus to discriminate sounds. The claim: it will "enrich your unborn child's forming cognitive, empathic, and creative skills."

Lured into the marketing copy, you can't help but wonder, "What if it really does work?" Save your money. No commercial product that claims to boost the braininess of a developing fetus has ever been scientifically proven to do anything useful.

Baby's needs are simple

Perhaps baby is too busy to bother with any interference from products. In the first half of pregnancy, baby starts creating her first brain cells—neurons—at the crazy rapid rate of 250,000 per minute. In the second half of pregnancy, the brain begins connecting those neurons, creating 700 synapses per second in the first few years of life. All baby needs at this stage is the nourishment you provide by eating well, exercising, and reducing your stress.

Bolster your friendships

We tend not to live near our families, and who pops over for tea anymore when there's txt msgs and Facebook?

We're increasingly isolated. But taking care of a baby is one thing you should not try to do alone. Parents need the emotional and practical support, and babies benefit from exposure to plenty of people. Social isolation can stress you and your marriage, in turn creating an environment harmful to baby.

You're going to need help. And it's up to you to make sure you get it.

You'll need friends to . . .
- bond with while your babies, preferably the same age, play together.
- watch baby while you sleep, shower, get a pedicure, or just do whatever.
- bring you dinner in the early weeks, when you won't want meals to involve much more than finding a fork.
- babysit, so you and your partner can have a regular date night.
- join you for girls' night or guys' night.

Apart from your existing friends, family, and neighbors, where can you find these people?

Plan dates with other parents-to-be from your childbirth education class.

Join a social group for new parents on meetup.com.

Ask around your neighborhood. You might be surprised by the number of resources for new parents. My neighborhood, for example, has a message-board group for parents, a yoga studio with prenatal and mom & baby classes, a café with a baby play area, a children's museum, classes for parents (breastfeeding, babywearing, bitch sessions), classes for babies (music, movement, swimming, story time at the library), new-parent support groups, and parents' nights out hosted by churches, community centers, and baby gyms. Before baby, I didn't know most of these existed.

Talk to strangers. Strike up a conversation with another parent or parent-to-be at the park or grocery store—as simple as "Aww, how old is your baby? What is she doing these days?" or "How are you holding up?" Share something honest. Don't pretend everything's perfect and perpetuate the unrealistic expectations we place on ourselves. Then, don't leave without exchanging contact info: "Hey, let me give you my e-mail address."

TRY THIS

Before baby, invite your dearest friends over for a cooking party, and stock up on freezer-friendly meals. Nourishingmeals.com has ideas for new moms.

As your due date nears, sign up with an online meal registry. This is a huge help in organizing the visitors who, bless them, offer to bring you hot meals.

Eating for two?
Not exactly

When you're pregnant, everyone wants you to eat a lot.

"Are you having a craving?" my husband would ask eagerly, ready to make a late-night snack run. "Here, finish these," friends ordered, pushing the fries in my direction. "Go for it," colleagues said as I went for seconds or thirds. "You're eating for two!"

Eventually a couple things sank in:

- You may be eating for two, but one of you is very, very small.
- You need only 300 extra calories a day in the first trimester. And only 350 extra in the second trimester. (That's one eight-grain roll at Starbucks.) And only 450 extra calories in the third. (A couple of oranges with your roll.)

A better way to think of "eating for two"
Focus instead on providing baby with two key nutrients:

Folic acid
What it does: cuts risk of neural tube defects by 76 percent

What it is: vitamin B9

How to get it: leafy greens (spinach, asparagus, turnip greens, lettuce), legumes (beans, peas, lentils), sunflower seeds, prenatal vitamins

When to eat it: four weeks before conception and during the first four weeks of pregnancy

Omega-3s
What they do: aid normal brain development. Babies whose moms got enough omega-3s (300 mg of DHA per day) were better at memory, recognition, attention, and fine motor skills at 6 months old.

What they are: essential fatty acids (ALA, DHA, and EPA), part of the membranes that make up a neuron

How to get them: Eat at least twelve ounces per week of oily fish with low concentrations of mercury. Flaxseed oil isn't converted by the body efficiently enough. Algae-derived DHA capsules (600 mg per day) have potential but are less studied.

When to eat them: Now. Then keep it up.

THE RESEARCH

In a study of twelve thousand women, the less seafood women ate during pregnancy, the greater their risk of having children with verbal IQs in the lowest quartile at 8 years old; behavioral problems at 7 years old; and poor social, communication, and fine motor skills in the early years.

The researchers concluded that any mercury you'd ingest from twelve ounces of fish per week is much less problematic than missing out on the omega-3s from the fish.

"We recorded no evidence to lend support to the warnings of the US advisory that pregnant women should limit their fish consumption," the researchers wrote.

less mercury	more mercury
Salmon	Swordfish
Shrimp	King mackerel
Sardines	Tilefish
Scallops	Shark
Catfish	
Pollock	
Tuna	

Exercise
thirty minutes a day

If you work out, keep it up. If you don't work out, start.

Doctors used to tell pregnant women to go easy on the exercise. Turns out they were being conservative because so few studies had been done on exercise during pregnancy.

More recent research shows that exercise is so beneficial, it outweighs the miniscule potential risk to baby's health. Signs of risk to the baby don't even begin to show up until you're exercising at a level that feels like an all-out sprint.

THE EFFECT OF EXERCISE ON BABY	
Exercise intensity	What happens to baby
Moderate or vigorous *(20 minutes of swimming, walking or running four-plus days a week)*	Baby's heart rate, breathing rate, and umbilical blood flow increase nicely along with yours
Strenuous *(A heart rate at 90% or more of maximum; athletes who are used to pushing their bodies very hard)*	Baby's heart rate and umbilical blood flow dip—but return to normal within 2½ minutes

Benefits for mom and baby
Exercise benefits the brain, not just the body:

- Exercise increases blood flow, which stimulates the body to make more blood vessels. More blood vessels give the brain more access to oxygen and energy.
- Aerobic exercise also increases BDNF (brain-derived neurotrophic factor), a chemical that grows new neurons. BDNF helps keep existing neurons going by making them less susceptible to damage and stress.
- BDNF karate-chops the toxic effects of stress hormones, including cortisol. In turn, baby's stress-response system and limbic system can develop normally.

Cardio beats weights

Strength training doesn't affect the brain like aerobic exercise does. A combination is great, but if you're pressed for time and energy, go with aerobic exercise. Swimming tops the list. The water supports your weight and disperses excess heat from your belly. The exercise works your entire body. Even if you're just bouncing along in the pool during senior swim, you'll feel so much better. Your impressively swollen ankles will, too.

Listen to your body

How much exercise is too much? Not enough research has been done to know for sure. Maybe that's why everyone says: Listen to your body.

I thought pregnant women weren't supposed to go running or bicycling, so I cut back on exercise when I got pregnant. Soon, I didn't feel healthy. Mid-pregnancy, I went back to my active lifestyle, respecting my mood in terms of how intensely I exercised. I felt so much better. For me, around eight months pregnant was the right time to scale back and just stroll around the neighborhood.

THE RESEARCH

Pregnant women—not used to working out—began exercising four times a week for forty-five to sixty minutes at a time. They started at about 12 weeks pregnant and continued through 36 weeks, doing things like hilly walks and step aerobics. Compared with women who didn't exercise, the exercisers were more fit, fewer had C-sections, and they recovered more quickly after delivery. In another study, women who were 28–32 weeks pregnant ran on a treadmill to exhaustion, and the babies experienced only a brief blip in heart rate and blood flow.

 DO IT NOW   What will you do for exercise?
Be specific about the day and time.

Sing or read to your belly

Newborns can recognize a song or story they heard in the womb.

In a quiet place, pregnant women read a three-minute story excerpted from *The Cat in the Hat* by Dr. Seuss. The women read out loud twice a day for the last six weeks of pregnancy.

After the babies were born, researchers gave them pacifiers attached to machines that could measure their sucking. Stronger sucking triggered audio of their mother reading the story. Weaker sucking triggered audio of her reading an unfamiliar story. The newborns sucked more strongly. They wanted to hear their story! (Or, at least, its familiar rhythms and intonations.)

Your baby, too, likely will find familiar words or songs to be soothing. You can try reciting them as soon as baby arrives.

While you're still pregnant, don't bother reciting anything to baby until your third trimester. Before that, baby can't hear you.

BILLIONS OF BERRIES FOR BLACKBERRY JAMBLE

My husband read *Jamberry*, by Bruce Degen, each night to my belly in the last couple months of my pregnancy. Turns out baby can't really hear dad's voice before birth. (We didn't know!) Mom's voice—resonating through and amplified by her body—is what baby can hear over the din of whooshes, sloshes, gurgles, and heartbeats in the womb. Still, my husband's reading provided a lovely bonding time for us. And the book became a favorite bedtime story for baby.

DO IT NOW Which song will you sing? Which book will you read?

Stress less

Are you thinking you'll move to a new city, start an intense new job, buy a new house, and finish remodeling just days before your new baby is born?

Here's a better idea: weekly massages, lazy weekend mornings, and dinners spent laughing with friends.

That's because toxic stress during the last few months of pregnancy transfers directly to baby. Excessive stress can

- make baby more irritable and less consolable;
- inhibit baby's motor skills, attention, and ability to concentrate;
- damage baby's stress-response system, causing fight-or-flight hormones to stick around too long; and
- shave an average of eight points off baby's IQ (the difference between average and bright).

How to identify toxic stress
Not all stress is bad, of course. And not all people react to the same stress in the same way. For example, at nine months pregnant, I was racing to finish editing a book. I found the late nights, tight deadlines, and clashing personalities invigorating. Friends thought I was crazy.

The problem is when you feel you have no control over the things stressing you out. Unrelenting stress is the main culprit. Our bodies just aren't built to handle a sustained assault of fight-or-flight stress hormones. An overly demanding job, a chronic illness, poverty, losing a job, an abusive relationship—these are examples of toxic stress.

Pregnancy does create a buffer against stress. Women, pregnant and not, were exposed to the same stressor, and the pregnant women had lower heart rates and cortisol levels. But if you're experiencing chronic stress or anxiety, especially starting in the second trimester, make it a priority to remedy your situation.

If you can't manage to lower your stress during pregnancy, focus on creating a trusting relationship with your newborn baby (see page 42). This has been shown to mitigate the effects of prenatal stress.

THE RESEARCH

Ice storm babies fall behind

When a freezing rain fell on eastern Canada in 1998, more than a million people lost electricity for up to forty days, and a hundred thousand families were shuttled into emergency shelters.

Women who were pregnant during all this were, understandably, stressed in a toxic way. It turns out their children were, too: at age 5½, the kids had lower IQs and poorer language abilities than kids whose mothers weren't affected by the storm.

DO IT NOW

List any areas causing you toxic stress. What big or small steps can you take to regain control?

What will you do for yourself to reduce stress in general?

Share the chores equally

Women in two-income households still do most of the work around the house.

This imbalance is a major minefield that new parents face, especially because baby brings so many new chores. It's also one of the most frequently cited sources of marital conflict. Find a fair solution, and it might save your marriage. (Hey, it might even improve your sex life. A study of nearly seven thousand couples found that as men's share of the weekly housework increases, couples have sex a little more often.)

Bottom line: if you're both working outside the home, household duties need to be shared fairly.

Gay couples are much better at this than straight couples, studies show, because they don't fall back on the assumptions that come with traditional gender roles. They have to start from scratch and divvy up every single task.

This is what we all need to do, too.

A ton of work

My husband and I were pretty surprised by the increase in housework that came with having a baby. This may be because, focused on our careers, we had done as little of it as possible. For example, we used to do laundry every two weeks, if we felt like it. Baby's cloth diapers and major spit-up habit meant we suddenly found ourselves doing laundry every two days.

We used to dirty one or two pans for dinner—if we weren't eating out. Plenty of nights we'd cook some pasta, stir in some spinach, and open a jar of sauce. Or toss a pizza in the oven. When baby started eating solid foods, I spent a lot more time cooking fresh produce, beans, and grains. Suddenly we were cleaning a whole pile of kitchen gear every night.

Not to mention wiping off and sweeping up food smeared on the table and dropped on the floor three meals a day. Or picking up toys and the contents of drawers constantly strewn across the house. Or making sure the floors were passably clean, since baby spent so much time on them.

You get the point. Housework goes from "if we get to it" weekly to "must be done" several times daily.

So you can imagine how resentment will quickly build if one person shoulders an unfair amount of that work.

Work vs. free time
(Both parents working)

Women   Men

32 HOURS	21 HOURS	
39 HOURS	45 HOURS	
25 HOURS	31 HOURS	

Housework & child care   Paid work   Free time

Who will do which chores?

People tend to be satisfied with their contribution to household work—and dissatisfied with their partner's contribution, studies show. And both parties feel underappreciated. So putting things down on paper is a clear, data-driven way to get on the same page.

With your partner, write down the household tasks each of you is responsible for, or use the list at right as inspiration. If the list is lopsided, decide how to balance it. One strategy is to claim chores you're each good at or don't mind doing. Compromise on the rest: flip a coin, trade off, or do them together.

Doing some chores together (say, one person cooks the main dish and the other makes the sides, or both of you clean at the same time) is good for your relationship, too.

FIRST SHIFT, SECOND SHIFT, THIRD SHIFT

The house turns into such a wreck each day, my husband and I made a pact. He would clean the house in the morning, after feeding baby breakfast and playing, so I wasn't starting the day with a mess. I would clean the house before he returned from work, so he wasn't coming home to chaos. Then we would tidy up together after dinner. When we stick to our plan, we find that our moods improve, and so do our attitudes toward each other.

TRY THIS

One quick way to make sure you're left doing most of the work is to continually criticize your partner's help. Cut each other some slack. Just say, "Thanks. I really appreciate that you put the dishes in the dishwasher." If you've been critical for years (ahem), it may take months for your partner to notice the change. Keep going.

Chore	Mine	Yours
Dishes	○	○
Meals		
Grocery shopping	○	○
Breakfast	○	○
Lunch	○	○
Dinner	○	○
Laundry		
Washing & drying	○	○
Folding & putting away	○	○
Garbage, recycling, compost	○	○
Bathrooms	○	○
Vacuuming	○	○
Dusting	○	○
Repairs	○	○
Paying bills	○	○
Scheduling the calendar	○	○
Getting baby ready to leave	○	○
Packing/unpacking diaper bag	○	○
Putting baby to bed		
Naps	○	○
Nighttime	○	○
Caring for baby		
(feeding, changing diapers, playing)		
Weekdays		
Morning	○	○
Afternoon	○	○
Evening	○	○
Nighttime wakings	○	○
Weekends		
Morning	○	○
Afternoon	○	○
Evening	○	○
Nighttime wakings	○	○

If you're suffering, get help

Depression among new parents is more common than you might think, and not discussed as much as it should be.

Postpartum depression can hit both parents. And if one parent is depressed, it's more likely that the other will be, too. The exact cause of postpartum depression isn't known, but hormones, lack of sleep, and stress are thought to be contributing factors.

Depression affects baby's brain, too. Depressed parents are less responsive to their babies, and they engage less positively with their babies. At 9 months old, the babies are

- less social,
- not as good at regulating their behavior,
- more emotionally negative,
- more easily stressed.

Fortunately, postpartum depression is treatable. Sooner is better. And parents' bond with their babies will be turned around, too.

Ways to prepare

Find a therapist before baby comes, so you'll have a number to call if you need it. Ask your doctor, midwife, doula, or friends for a recommendation. You want someone who can see you immediately, not in six weeks.

Designate a close friend or family member, or both, to tell you if he or she sees symptoms of depression in you. You might not see symptoms in yourself.

When to get help

A couple weeks of "baby blues"—fatigue, sadness, and worry—are normal. But if you feel anxious and overwhelmed most of the time, for longer than two weeks, get help. No excuses. No judgment. For men, common symptoms include feeling tired and irritable, escaping (into work, sports, alcohol), or acting more controlling, aggressive, or reckless. For women, see the next page.

within first year

Both parents are vulnerable to depression

15%–20%
of moms

10%
of dads

peaks at
3-6 months

Do I have postpartum depression?

If you have had a baby within the last twelve months, and you have experienced some of these symptoms for more than two weeks, please find help. This list comes from Katherine Stone, publisher of PostpartumProgress.com, the most widely read blog on postpartum depression.

- You feel overwhelmed. Not like "Hey, this new-mom thing is hard." More like "I can't do this and I'm never going to be able to do this."

- You feel guilty because you believe you should be handling new motherhood better than this. You feel like your baby deserves better.

- You don't feel bonded to your baby. You're not having that mythical mommy bliss that you see on TV or read about in magazines.

- You continually feel irritated or angry. You have no patience. Everything annoys you. You feel resentment toward your baby, or your partner, or your friends who don't have babies. You feel out-of-control rage.

- You feel nothing but emptiness and numbness. You are just going through the motions.

- You feel sadness to the depths of your soul. You can't stop crying, even when there's no real reason to be crying.

- You can't bring yourself to eat, or perhaps the only thing that makes you feel better is eating.

- You can't sleep, no matter how tired you are. Or maybe all you can do is sleep. Whichever it is, your sleeping is completely screwed up, and it's not just because you have a newborn.

- You can't concentrate. You can't focus. You can't think of the words you want to say. You can't remember what you were supposed to do. You can't make a decision. You feel like you're in a fog.

- You feel disconnected. You feel strangely apart from everyone, like there's an invisible wall between you and the rest of the world.

- You might be having thoughts of running away and leaving your family behind.

- You've thought of driving off the road, or taking too many pills, or finding some other way to end this misery.

- You know something is wrong, that the way you are feeling is NOT right. You wonder if you've "gone crazy."

- You are afraid that this is your new reality and that you've lost the "old you" forever.

- You are afraid that if you reach out for help, people will judge you. Or that your baby will be taken away.

Used with permission

Expect conflict as a couple

Two-thirds of couples struggle with their marriages soon after baby arrives.

The majority of couples report a drop in marital satisfaction after baby. It hits its lowest point when the kids are teenagers, and it doesn't rebound until the kids move out.

Why is this important for baby? Because if you're stressed out and fighting—or headed toward divorce—you're creating a home environment that hurts your child's brain development.

A few factors put you at higher risk for a drop in marital satisfaction:

- If the mother's parents are divorced or had high levels of conflict
- If you lived together before getting married
- If you had a baby soon after getting married (waiting gives you more time to get on the same page about relationship responsibilities)
- If you have a lot of negative communication and didn't handle conflict well before baby
- If one of you didn't want a baby but caved in

Well, that covers just about all of us.

The good news

In a third of relationships, marital satisfaction stays the same or improves after baby. What are they doing right? They're choosing empathy (see page 136), dealing with conflicts lovingly (see page 138), sharing the chores (see page 18), and building a great support network (see page 8).

You can make a concerted effort to do these things, too.

The transition to parenthood is tough

Four studies of marital satisfaction ask different questions but arrive at similar answers.
Source: C. Walker, "Some Variations in Marital Satisfaction." Copyright Elsevier. Used with permission.

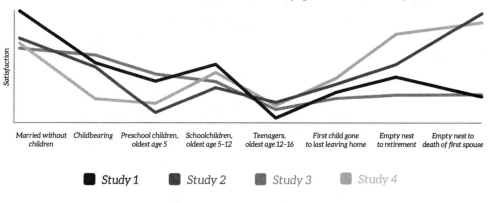

Know you can't truly be prepared

You're going to be clueless, and that's OK.

Having a baby is a culture shock. As much time as you spent planning for this, it all becomes real quite suddenly. You don't speak baby's language; you're not sure what she's trying to tell you. You feel incompetent when it comes to the most basic things, like how much this little human needs to eat or how she wants to sleep. You've never been in such close contact with spit-up, drool, pee, and poop—things you'd previously tried to avoid. You barely recognize your house, as cleaning falls to the wayside and baby stuff piles up. Your senses become heightened: you start to hear baby's cries when there are none, or you bolt upright in bed with the urge to make sure baby's still alive. Time ceases to have meaning. When baby cries inconsolably, minutes feel like hours. When you look into baby's eyes, cuddle, and kiss baby's soft skin, hours feel like minutes.

It's an adventure, and generally you feel up for it. Plus, baby sleeps a ton at first, giving you a little time to adjust.

However, many first-time parents also face an additional challenge that hits hard. It could be postpartum depression. It could be that baby is colicky, or underweight, or not latching at the breast, or premature. It could be that you're an ambitious person and haven't yet figured out that you're trying to do too much. For my husband and me, it was sleep deprivation.

Feeding baby was taking two hours—and you're supposed to feed a newborn at least every three hours. I wasn't producing much milk, but I didn't want to give up on breastfeeding. So the hospital had us taping a tiny tube to my breast, and passing milk through it using a syringe. That way, baby was still "nursing." Getting this tube to stay in place *and* getting baby to latch was indescribably time-consuming and frustrating. If baby let go, we'd have to start all over. Then switch breasts. Then I'd use a breast pump. Then my husband would sterilize all the equipment. We were reeling from lack of sleep.

My husband and I rarely fight, but suddenly we were arguing over critical things like whether the phrase "Don't cry over spilled milk" referred to the child or the mother. Emotions ran high or low, nothing in between. I remember walking down the street in broad daylight and bursting into tears. My husband blurted out, "Where are the *joys* of parenthood?" Within ten days, we ditched the syringe, switched to bottles, I pumped less often, and we caught up on sleep.

Gradually, we defined, then accepted, then embraced, our new normal as parents. Soon enough, we felt like we were getting the hang of things. And you will, too.

Not that parenting will suddenly become easy. With a baby, just about every day has highs and lows. Woven throughout moments of frustration, anxiety, and exhaustion are moments of such immense joy, strength, determination, humor, and love. These blissful times more than erase the hard ones.

I remember one sunny day when my baby was 7 or 8 months old. Walking through a beautiful forested park, I told her how the leaves had fallen from the trees. I sat in a swing with her facing me in my lap, and as we swung, she leaned against my chest and smiled a supremely content little smile. This made such happiness well up inside me that I laughed out loud, hugged her to me, and said, "I love you so much!"

Moments like these come from a deep connection with a person. You can feel it with friends or lovers occasionally, but with a child you get to feel it several times a day in such a pure sense. It makes you realize that's what's most important in life—our connections as humans.

Maybe this is why veteran parents forget to tell us first-timers how hard parenting can be. If so, it's a pretty good reason.

Envision baby all grown up

Take a moment to imagine your child as an adult.

What kind of work do you hope she is doing? What values do you hope he has? What life skills? What kind of relationship does your baby have with you, family, friends, and partners?

At first it might be difficult to imagine your baby being anything but a baby. It was for my husband and me. We did this exercise with Seattle-based parent coach Nita Talwar. Busy just keeping our heads above water, we spent more time worrying about baby's next nap than pondering what our child would be like twenty years from now. Quickly, though, I could see the power of looking ahead.

"It's easier to get where you want to go," Nita pointed out, "if you have a map."

Stating the skills and character traits that you value helps you prioritize how you want to parent. My husband and I each put "good communicator; articulate" on our lists—not surprising, given that we're both writers and editors. I'm naturally a listener rather than a talker, but I overrode my quiet tendencies to talk to our baby a lot (see page 52). If we hadn't stopped to think about what we value, I might have let that slide.

DO IT NOW Write down the values and life skills you hope your child exhibits as an adult, twenty or thirty years from now. How will you need to change in order to model those things?

Which brings up another point: you might have to grow, too

Do you hope your daughter has a loving, healthy relationship with her partner? Then you'll need to show her that kind of relationship. Do you hope she has empathy and respect for others? Then you'll need to model that.

Do you hope your son values helping others? Then you'll need to help others. Do you hope he knows how to solve problems in a calm way without being hurtful? Then you'll have to do so.

What image do you want your baby to have of what a good father or mother is? Then . . . you get the idea.

This might require making some changes in your life.

No one wants to hear that, right? Some days I think: I'm just doing the best I can, based on who I am. Other days, I'm surprised by my desire to become a better person for my baby.

TRY THIS

During any given wonderful or terrible moment, you think, "I'll remember this forever." You won't. That would require remembering nearly every single day of baby's life. If you're like me, you can barely remember what happened yesterday.

So, since pregnancy, I've kept a "One Line a Day" journal. One line per day is just about the right level of commitment. OK, one line every few days. Mine is a five-year journal: each page is devoted to one date, with space to write about each of the five years.

It's neat to be reminded of what was happening on a certain date in previous years— and to wonder what my baby will glean from the journal when she's all grown up.

Love

The most important thing you can do with your newborn is to be sensitive to baby's needs. Respond when baby tries to engage with you. Match those smiles, coos, and gazes. Comfort those cries. Cuddle up, skin to skin. Fall in love.

Prepare to be amazed

Babies' minds are working and working, testing hypotheses, and making use of an incredible set of innate cognitive abilities.

A newborn less than one hour old can imitate. Even though he's never seen a face before, including his own, a baby is born knowing how to stick out his tongue at you, if you stick out yours.

Babies shun the bad guy. Babies 6 and 10 months old watched a show in which one toy helps another toy up a hill. A third toy pushes it back down the hill. The researchers then brought in the helper toy and the hinderer toy for the babies to play with. Babies were much more likely to reach for the helper toy.

Babies can predict an action. When 9-month-olds reach for an object, their brain's motor region is activated. And when 9-month-olds simply watch an adult reach for an object, that same motor region is activated. Watching the adult a second time, the babies' motor region activates just prior to the adult reaching—in effect predicting the adult's action.

Babies can make predictions based on probability. Infants 10 to 12 months old were tested to see whether they preferred a pink lollipop or a black one. Next, babies were shown two jars: one with more pink lollipops and one with more black. Researchers then plucked a lollipop from each jar (shielded now, so baby couldn't tell which color lollipop was chosen) and covered each lollipop with a cup. About 80 percent of the time, the infants chose the cup most likely to contain their favorite color of lollipop.

Do something one time, and a 14-month-old can repeat it a week later in the same context. Researchers created a box that would light up when touched. As babies watched, experimenters leaned forward from the waist and touched their foreheads to the box. Brought back to the lab a week later, two-thirds of babies remembered. They leaned forward and touched their own foreheads to the box. The researchers tried longer delays, too—and some babies remembered *four months later.*

Babies will give you broccoli. An 18-month-old understands that your wants might differ from hers. In front of the child, an experimenter ate raw broccoli, making a happy face ("Mmm!"), and then goldfish crackers, making a disgusted face ("Yuck!"). Then the experimenter held out her hand to the child and said, "Could you give me some?" Even though they prefer crackers, 18-month-olds gave her raw broccoli—what the experimenter said she liked. The experiment also was done with 15-month-olds. Babies at that age always hand over crackers, which is what they like.

Babies are taking statistics. Babies take in everything from the environment around them—sounds, visual scenes, language—and calculate the frequency with which something occurs. In the case of language, babies use these statistics to determine which letter sounds to continue discriminating between and which to drop.

Babies are designed to learn. Babies absorb information from many sources at once, lighting up a host of neurotransmitters—many more than adult brains have—that leap into action for rapid learning. Then, like scientists, babies and young children create hypotheses and run experiments about the world and about human nature. Researcher Alison Gopnik calls young children "the research and development division of the human species."

SEE WHAT BABY CAN DO

I'm continually impressed by the things my baby can do, say, remember, and repeat. Before babies can talk, you tend to assume they don't understand anything you're saying. They do. Dressing my baby in a shirt at 10 months old, I asked her to put her arm in the sleeve—and she did. When baby started talking, it was too late to take back some of the things my husband and I had said to her. "Butt balm for the butt!" she'd repeat during diaper changes.

If I give baby enough time, patiently waiting instead of jumping in to help, she's often able to twist on a lid, snap a buckle, find a towel and wipe up a spill, or put away an item before moving on to the next thing. At 20 months old, I was surprised to learn she could finish the sentences of favorite books, if I paused. Reading *Corduroy*, about a small bear in green overalls who's missing a button, I'd start, "I didn't know I'd . . ." and she'd finish, "lost a button, said to self. I'll go FIND it!"

It's easy to underestimate a baby. Keep testing your baby's boundaries—and prepare to be amazed.

Create a feeling of safety

Yes, you should anchor your furniture to the walls and lock away your cleaning supplies. But that's not the kind of safety I mean here.

Your baby's strongest need is to feel safe with you.

Children are exquisitely sensitive to their environments. If you create an environment of safety, love, and emotional stability, good things happen:

- Baby's brain develops a healthy stress-response system, efficiently deploying and then reducing stress hormones as needed.
- With stress hormones in balance, baby's neural circuits for learning and reasoning are protected. The cardiovascular and immune systems can function properly.
- Life's smaller stresses ("No shirt! I don't *want* it!") become chances for growth, because supportive relationships buffer the negative effects of stress.
- Baby sees your healthy responses to stressful experiences and gets practice responding in healthy ways.

In a home with high levels of conflict, on the other hand, baby's stress-response system is damaged. The system is either forced into a state of constant high alert or dulled into reacting too mildly to stress. Baby is unable to form a trusting attachment with caregivers (see page 42). Later, the child is more likely to be aggressive and delinquent. You might think babies are too young to understand that their parents are fighting. But babies younger than 6 months old can tell something is wrong. Babies' blood pressure and heart rate rise, and so do their levels of the stress hormone cortisol.

How you fight matters

That doesn't mean you can never fight. Not all parents' fights hurt a child's brain development. If, when you argue, you are supportive of your partner and show small signs of affection (see page 138), children learn that you can and will manage conflict in a way that preserves family harmony. If you are hostile with your partner, making threats and lobbing insults, or you're physically aggressive, that's when the conflicts harm kids.

Baby's stress-response system develops over the first year

The kinds of things that stress baby (that is, increase her cortisol level) change as experiences fine-tune baby's stress-response system.

Newborn	Cortisol increases even if baby is picked up
3 months	Being picked up is no longer stressful, but a doctor exam is
6 months	Cortisol is less reactive during a doctor exam and shots
9 months	Being left with a trusted babysitter barely increases cortisol
13 months	Baby can be upset with no increase in cortisol

Comfort newborn with the familiar

Thrust into a foreign place, who wouldn't be comforted by the vestiges of home?

Newborns cry because they're hungry or gassy or sleepy or hot or cold or wet. And they cry after you've checked all those things, for reasons that will remain a mystery. Baby's dealing with a lot right now. You can't always solve the problem to stop the crying, but you can comfort baby as he cries.

Scent

Researchers recorded the crying of newborns, a mere 30 minutes old, who were separated from their mothers for an hour. If the babies were exposed to the smell of the mother's amniotic fluid—the protective sac of water baby had been floating in before birth—they cried less than thirty seconds. If not, they cried more than two minutes.

What else is a familiar scent to a newborn? Well, mom, for one. Baby can smell you starting at seven months in the womb—your body odor, even the lotion you rub on your belly each evening. (Might I recommend Almond Supple Skin Oil from L'Occitane? Mmm. Drop hints for your baby shower.) Soon after birth, dad's scent can become familiar, too.

During the painful heel prick to draw baby's blood, babies cried and grimaced much less if they smelled a familiar scent. Mama's milk worked for breastfed babies. The scent of vanilla, which researchers previously had wafted under baby's nose, worked as well.

Sound

If you sang or read to baby during your third trimester of pregnancy (see page 14), use that song or story to comfort baby right after birth.

Motion

Wrap baby to your body and walk (see page 206)—a very familiar cadence to baby.

Sniff, sniff? Newborns cry less

Median crying time during separation from mom, when exposed to her amniotic fluid vs. no exposure.

Exposed — **29** SECONDS

Not exposed — **135** SECONDS

GOOD TO KNOW

Babies are often able to self-calm if given time. Before running over to bounce and pat away a cry, run through Patty Wipfler's acronym CALMS:

Check in with your feelings (we're often the ones stressed out).
Allow yourself a breath.
Listen to your baby's cries.
Mirror what you hear with empathy ("You are sooo upset").
Soothe as the last step.

For persistent crying, Harvey Karp's "Five S's" can work beautifully to comfort baby: swaddling, side or stomach position, swinging, shushing, and sucking. Videos at happiestbaby.com show you exactly how.

Cuddle with baby

Babies are happy with almost constant contact in their first few months. Touch feels good!

Affectionate touch is essential for cognitive and emotional development. More technically: touch triggers the release of certain neurotransmitters, which soothe the nervous system and lower baby's levels of cortisol, a stress hormone. Touch signals safety to the brain.

At the extreme negative end, babies not touched for days on end simply stare off into space. Their stress-response system is damaged, creating a cascade of negative effects.

Ways to get close

In baby's first weeks, you're in a haze just trying to get the hang of all this feeding, burping, napping, pooping, and generally keeping baby alive. Then, at some point in the day, all of those things have occurred, and you may wonder: Now what do we do?

Instead of setting baby in a swing to stare at mobiles, cuddle up:

Go skin to skin. Let your newborn, wearing only a diaper, rest on mom's or dad's bare chest. Snuggle with baby in bed the same way. Breastfeed topless at home. Your skin warms baby, but you can also put a blanket over the two of you. Being skin to skin, or nursing, when the doctor gives baby heel pricks or shots also lowers baby's stress.

Wrap baby against your body. Use a soft-structured carrier, sling, or wrap while you run your errands, do some chores, or go for a walk. (After you've recovered from the labor, I mean—don't go anywhere at first, if you can help it!) Save the stroller for when baby gets heavy or you need to haul stuff.

Massage baby each day. Researchers found that 4-month-olds who got a daily eight-minute massage were

- in a better mood,
- less anxious and stressed,
- more attentive, and
- sleeping more regularly.

Seems to me like massage does the same for moms . . .

Start with baby on his back, then his tummy. The pressure needs to be moderate, not too light. In India, where baby massage is a centuries-old tradition, women lay baby on their outstretched legs and work vigorously with warm oil. (Search online for a video to get an idea of the amount of pressure.) Talk to, sing to, or smile at baby while you massage. A silent, distant massage only raises baby's stress level. If baby seems agitated, adjust your touch, or try another time—baby may just need a break right now (see page 42).

THE RESEARCH

In one study, preterm babies got skin-to-skin contact ("kangaroo care") each day. Each time researchers followed up, between 6 months old and 10 years old, these babies had more efficient stress responses, more organized sleep patterns, and better executive function than preterm babies cared for in an incubator. The new moms were less anxious, too.

Get in sync

....

Baby loves it when you mimic her facial expressions, coo at her little sounds, and gaze into her eyes.

When baby tries to engage with you in one of those ways, she needs you to respond in kind. This "serve and return" interaction is foundational in wiring baby's brain. It helps the brain develop in a way that supports stress regulation, empathy, and emotional stability. But sometimes baby needs a break.

I was leaning over my newborn on a play mat, laughing and cooing, when baby suddenly turned her head to the left, lost in a million-mile stare. I had an urge to say, "Hello? Where'd you go?"

Then I remembered that when a baby is overstimulated, she tells you by

- turning her head away,
- closing her eyes,
- avoiding your gaze,
- tensing up, or
- suddenly becoming fussy.

It was neat for me to understand what was happening. And it helped me resist my initial urge to bring baby back by calling her name or waving in front of her face. My baby turned back to me just a few moments later, ready to carry on.

Synchrony creates a trusting relationship

Matching baby's lulls by patiently waiting, and then engaging when she does, is a hallmark of responsive, sensitive parenting. You're attuned to baby, aware of baby's cues, and quick to respond to baby's cues. Sensitive parenting helps baby form a trusting relationship with you, called "secure attachment." Parents who continually ignore or reject their baby's bids for interaction and reassurance don't create a trusting relationship. Attachment has nothing to do with whether baby is constantly attached to your body.

Being out of sync stresses baby

When mama and baby are in sync, their biological rhythms are, too. For example, during face-to-face interaction, their heartbeats become coordinated with a lag of less than one second.

When parent and baby are out of sync, baby gets stressed. Harvard researcher Ed Tronick conducted "still face" experiments in which mothers simply gave a blank stare when their babies wanted to engage. The babies tried smiling, pointing, waving, and screeching, all to no avail. Babies then began to turn away, cry, and slump. When the mothers quit their act, it took their babies a moment to trust them again and reengage. But they did reengage. Building (or breaking) a trusting relationship with baby is a process that happens over several years.

EXAMPLES OF ATTACHMENT	
Secure attachment	**Insecure attachment**
Child turns to you for protection and comfort	Child turns away from you when distressed
Child uses you as a base from which to explore the world	Child alternates between clinging and pushing you away

Smile, hug, encourage

A smile, a wink, a hug, or a word of encouragement helps create a positive home environment. When children get attention in positive ways, they are less likely to seek attention in negative ways.

Include baby

Quality time with baby can mean taking out the garbage together.

Including baby in life's little tasks requires accepting that any task will take much, much longer. But that's OK. Engaging baby in whatever you're doing gives you lots to show baby and lots to talk about, along with little moments you'll cherish.

For part of the day, baby and I have friends to meet, books to read, music to dance to, and walks to go on. But when I need to get stuff done, here are some of the things that work for me:

Showering

- Before baby can sit up: Cradle baby in a portable chair, or surround baby with pillows on the floor within your view.
- Once baby can sit up: Let baby splash, too, on the bathtub floor or in a bucket-style baby bath. I'm very grateful for our Tummy Tub.

Cooking

- Before baby can sit up, put baby in a carrier.
- Prep food at the dining-room table while baby sits in the high chair, or bring the high chair to the kitchen. Talk about all of the ingredients, and pass baby produce to feel or taste.
- Sit baby on the floor with some blocks, pans and utensils, or food samples. Explain the things you're doing.
- Get a stool or "learning tower" so your child can see. Have her help, by throwing away packaging, pouring ingredients into the pot, or stirring.
- I often make a green smoothie in the blender. Baby likes to nibble the pear, twist the lemon halves on the citrus juicer, strip the stems from the kale, and watch everything whirl. As I turn on the blender, I say, "Loud noise in one, two, three—" and we do a little dance.

≫

«

Laundry

- Let baby put a couple items in the machine, twist some knobs, and watch the spinning clothes—it's TV for babies!
- Play peekaboo while folding laundry.
- Ask your toddler to put away items that belong in his room.
- Make the bed with baby in it. Whip the sheet into the air and let it float down over the two of you.

Cleaning

- Hand over part of the job. Around 18 months, my baby liked to get out the dustpan when I was sweeping, and she'd grab the rag to wipe up spills.
- Enlist baby's help to empty the dishwasher: "Here, put your dish on your shelf. Can you get your stool, and put your spoon in the drawer?"

Fixing stuff

- Your toddler would probably love to help you assemble her new balance bike, remove the old knobs from the dresser drawers, or sit in your suitcase and twist the screwdriver to tighten the handle. Explain as you go.

Errands

- Walk, if you can, or take the bus. People you pass by love to talk with baby, and you see all sorts of interesting things.
- Choose one errand and make a day of it. For example, I once walked to a store five miles away. Baby and I had plenty to look at along the way, we ran into a friend, we stopped for lunch, and we took the bus home. The errand took hours, technically, but it made for a nice day.

Talk

*Describe the world to baby in all its richness.
"Mmm, pomegranate seeds. Aren't they a beautiful color? A deep red, like rubies." Count the stairs
as you walk them. Recount your day. Say anything
and everything—just talk a ton. Read every day.*

Speak in a singsongy voice

The best way to talk with baby is to snuggle in close and use a high, lilting voice with drawn-out vowels.

It's called "parentese." In the first eighteen months, it helps baby pick out and imitate parts of language.

That's because each vowel and word becomes more distinct, so they're easier for baby to discern. The higher pitch matches the limited range of a baby's smaller vocal tract—one-quarter the size of yours.

It's not what you say, it's how you say it

Speak directly to baby, one-on-one, when possible. Make it a conversation. (Take turns, pausing to let baby respond with a coo, gaze, or gesture.)

In a recent study, babies who heard more "one-on-one parentese" shot ahead of the others in language development. Around age 1, they babbled more than babies who heard less one-on-one parentese. When the tots turned 2, parents checked off a list of 680 words (a standard inventory) to report how many words their children spoke.

Babies who had heard the most one-on-one parentese had more than double the vocabulary of those who had heard the least: 433 words vs. 168 words.

Infants prefer the pitch of parentese to adult speech, according to decades of research:

- Babies' heart rates increased when they heard parentese, even in a foreign language.
- At 5 months old, babies smiled more at approvals and looked worried at disapprovals in parentese.
- At 12 months old, babies asked to look at a picture did so more often when asked in parentese.

Researchers, led by Nairán Ramírez-Esparza and Patricia Kuhl, recorded 26 families' conversations in their homes. (Usually families are brought into a lab, a less natural setting.)

They recorded 8-hour stretches on each of four days. (The unobtrusive recordings were courtesy of LENA, a lightweight recorder that snaps into a shirt pocket and comes with speech-analysis software.)

So the researchers had access to interactions that researchers usually don't get, plus the ability to study the social context of each interaction.

TRY THIS

Read a magazine story to your baby, using the same tone and speed you would with your partner. See how your baby reacts. (Mine tries to pinch my lips closed.) Now read it again in parentese.

It's pretty funny to look baby in the eyes and say, wide-eyed and smiling, something like, "Unfortunately, encounters with cops are always at the worst moments in your life." But watch baby engage!

Talk to your baby a ton

If your baby hears a ton of talk in her first three years, she'll have a bigger vocabulary, a higher IQ, and better grades than children who aren't talked to much.

When should you start? In the last ten weeks of pregnancy. Babies begin to absorb language, as the mother's voice reverberates through her body, earlier than researchers realized.

Talk richly

Simplify a description or explanation, but there's no need to avoid using the proper words. Most words are unusual to a baby, right? Instead of just "Look—airplane!" you might say, "That's a *seaplane*. Do you see how the plane has two feet? Those feet are called pontoons. Pontoons let the plane float on the water. A seaplane floats on the water." (To such explanations, my baby replies amenably, "OK, yeah.")

Talk positively

Encourage your child. "Wow, you're learning to pour! Oops, the water spilled. Yeah, it's tricky to line up the cups. We'll clean that up. OK, let's try again—hold your hand here . . ." That's more encouraging than saying, "Let Daddy pour that. You're going to spill it."

Repeat or rephrase baby's words.
"Ball! Yes, you're playing with a ball."

Give positive feedback.
Use more "That works" and "That's it" than "Don't," "Stop," and "Bad." Point out strengths. "You are persistent." "That shows you are creative." (See page 176.)

Use directives to direct and questions to give choices.
Leave out the "OK?" at the end when you don't intend to offer a choice.

Talk directly to baby
Speech that baby simply overhears doesn't provide the same boost in baby's vocabulary or language proficiency. Neither does playing audio or video of someone talking. The brain is electrified by face-to-face interaction, so much so that the presence or absence of that social connection acts as a gate to learning language.

Talk regularly
Children who are talked to more often get a brain boost. It helps to have places to go and people to see, which gives you a world of things to describe and explain. (See page 45 for more ideas.)

Say anything and everything

Newborn and infant

It may feel a little strange to talk this much to someone who doesn't talk back. But you get used to it.

Read out loud. A newspaper story, for example, gives you a chance to catch up on the world (if you can keep baby from ripping the paper and eating it).

Explain what's about to happen to baby. Babies understand more than you think they do, and it helps to give them a little notice before moving them this way and that. "Let's change your diaper. Here comes a wet wipe. Legs up . . . legs down." "I'm going to put on your hat, and then we'll walk outside." "Grandma is going to visit you today."

Narrate your day—whatever you're doing, seeing, thinking, and feeling. Take moments to engage your baby with eye contact, a smile, or a tickle. It doesn't really matter what you talk about.

Examples

Folding laundry: "Oh good, two matching socks. *Two matching socks!* I'm folding the tops together so one doesn't get lost. There we go." "Ooh, a nice warm sheet." (Cover baby's head, then lift it away.) "Where's baby? There's baby!"

Going for a walk: Talk about where you're going today and what you see as you pass by.

Dressing baby: "Let's see, which shirt will you wear today? I'm partial to this one. Over the head!" (Baby flips over and wiggles away.) "Come here, little fishy. We're not done yet!" (Scoot baby back to you with kisses.) "Left arm through. Right arm through. Good. Well, aren't you cute. Aren't you cute!"

Making a bottle: "Fill . . . scoop . . . pour . . . twist . . . shake-shake-shake."

Toddler

Once baby is more active, all this talking gets easier and, I found, feels less silly—even if it doesn't sound less silly.

Examples

Simply describe all the impressive stuff baby is doing. "You opened the drawer. You closed the drawer. Open. Close. Open. Close. You did it! You're pulling the drawer open. You're pushing the drawer closed. Pull. Push. Pull. Push. Ooh, a pen. You found a pen in the drawer. Wow, you took the lid off the pen! I'll take that . . ."

Explain whatever baby seems interested in. "Yes, that's Daddy's helmet. HEL-met. He's putting it on his head. He's buckling the strap under his chin. Now he can safely ride his bike."

Build nouns into sentences. "Lid. This is a lid. A lid goes on top of a pan. I put the lid on top of the pan. Can you put the lid on top of the pan?"

Once baby starts talking, interacting this way becomes even more fun—and impossibly cute. Before you know it, baby starts repeating everything you say. Then you can teach baby to say things you want to hear. Our baby says, "Daddy runs fast!" and "Go, Pack, go!"

> (**DO IT NOW**) Which situations will you narrate to baby?

2,100 words per hour?!

Betty Hart tried everything she could think of to improve the vocabularies of the 4-year-olds in the low-income preschool where she was teaching. She couldn't do it. Finally, she and Todd Risley, her graduate supervisor at the University of Kansas, figured out that, by age 4, it was too late.

They wanted to know why.

So they followed forty-two families and recorded every word they said—for one hour per month, over two-and-a-half years.

It took six years to transcribe the resulting thirteen hundred hours of tapes. Hart and Risley then analyzed the differences in the way rich and poor parents speak with their children. They studied the quality of the talking from many angles: Did the mix of nouns and verbs matter? The vocabulary level? Whether the talk was positive or negative?

The number of words turned out to be the most interesting variable:

- A child in a family on welfare heard an average of 600 words an hour, while a child in a professional family heard 2,100 words an hour.
- By age 4, children of professional parents had heard forty-eight million words addressed to them; children in poor families had heard thirteen million. No wonder poor kids were behind in vocabulary and speech acquisition—differences that affected their later educational abilities.
- Children's language skills at age 3 predicted their language skills at age 9 or 10.

How much is the "ton of talk" baby needs to hear to have a bigger vocabulary, a higher IQ, and better grades? Researchers found that it's 21,000 words a day, or 2,100 words an hour. Sound daunting? I thought so at first.

As it turns out, 2,100 words an hour does not mean a stream of constant chatter. It's about fifteen minutes' worth of talking over an hour.

Parents also tend to speak in chunks averaging only four words: "Hi, beautiful baby." "Who's that in the mirror? Is that you?" "Oops, Mommy forgot her keys." "Where are your shoes?" Simple phrases—they count. These parents weren't riffing on the theory of relativity.

In the study, professional families averaged 487 of these utterances per hour. Low-income families averaged 176 per hour.

Vocab explosion!

Age	Average child can understand
1½ years	100 words
3 years	1,000 words
6 years	6,000 words (only 44,000 more to go . . .)

A LITTLE TEST AT THE SINK: 60 WORDS TAKES 26 SECONDS

OK, let's wash your hands. This is the cold water. No, that's the hot water. We'll put a little soapy on your palm. Yep, rub, rub, rub. You're rubbing your hands together. Ooh, I see lots of bubbles. Let's get the backs of your hands. Good. OK, time to rinse! Rub, rub, rub under the water. All right, let's dry.

Read together

....

Look at the words on the page and say them out loud. That's how one reads a book to a child, I assumed. Nope.

Babies & babblers

Before 6 months
Think of "reading" more as exploring the concept of books. Read sturdy board books, and let baby chew corners. Or read aloud whatever magazine or novel you're into at the moment (or were into, before baby). This way, you'll be exposing baby to the sounds of language and getting a break from "all things baby."

6–12 months
Talk about the pictures. Encourage baby to point: "Where's the yellow flower?" Let baby turn pages and feel textures. Baby doesn't care much about the plot at this point. Don't feel like you have to finish the book.

12–18 months
Engage baby with dramatic readings, different voices, big expressions, and gestures. When a bee goes "buzz!" you can make the sound and come in close to land a kiss. When a character goes fast or slow, you can use your fingertips to crawl or run up baby's belly.

Read together every day, even if just for five or ten minutes.

TRY THIS

Find a picture book with few words. For example, in Good Night, Gorilla, *each page says little more than "Good night." Flotsam has no words at all. Without a written narrative to fall back on, you have to make up a story based on the pictures.*

Talkers

1½ years–3 years

Help your child become the storyteller. Each time you read the same book, do less reading yourself, and let your child talk more. You point, label objects, and ask questions. Children's oral language skills improved, one study found, after fifteen weeks of this interactive style of reading.

The Stony Brook Reading and Language Project, led by researcher Grover Whitehurst, developed the "PEER sequence" to summarize the fairly natural and brief exchange:

- **PROMPT your child to say something about the book:** "What is this?" (pointing to bird)
- **EVALUATE your child's response:** (child says "bird") "That's right!"
- **EXPAND on your child's response** by rephrasing it or adding information to it: "It's a blackbird."
- **REPEAT a prompt about the expansion:** "Can you say blackbird?"

When baby first starts talking, ask him to name objects. "What is that?"

Later, ask what, when, where, and why prompts: "When does the moon come out?" "Where are all the animals going?" "What is that sneaky gorilla doing?"

As your child is able to answer those, ask open-ended questions: "What's happening in this picture?"

You want to use the PEER sequence on almost every page, Whitehurst says, after you've read through the book once or twice.

≫

«

1½ years–3 years

Read alphabet books and rhymes. Both teach children about phonemes, the sounds of letters. Choose alphabet books that show several things starting with the same letter ("C is a crab with two clamping claws") and rhyming books ("Today I say! Without delay!"). As you're reading, pause so that your child can finish the sentence: "And the noisy, nasty nuisance grew, 'til the villagers cried ___ [What can we do?]"

Sound out words, syllable by syllable. This helps children link letters and their sounds, necessary for decoding words and for spelling. At this stage, your child learns to name a letter and make the sound of that letter, can tell you a word that rhymes with another word, and knows you've said "cat" if you make the sounds /k/ and /at/.

4–5 years

Have your child read aloud. Point out what they know along the way. This significantly improves word recognition, fluency, and comprehension—both for good and not-so-good readers, and across ages.

Relate an event in the story to real life: "We saw a boat yesterday." "You've felt frustrated like that, too." (Statements instead of questions put kids in the lead, says parent coach Sandy Blackard. "Pointing out what they know meets kids' need for power," she says, "and makes reading more fun.")

Ask questions about the story while you read. Reread parts that your child didn't understand. After the story—or before reading it yet again—ask a question about the plot: "Did Franklin want a dog for a pet? How did his parents react?" Have your child come up with his own questions about the story. Research hints that the conversation during reading is more important than the actual reading.

Reading isn't just pleasurable, it's necessary. It opens our minds to new ideas and possibilities; it informs and, sometimes, it inspires. It's a lovely way for you and your child to bond with each other.

Reading also presents by far the best opportunity to learn new words. We're not all that expansive when we talk. Children's books tend to use almost twice as many unusual words as college-educated adults do in conversation. A larger vocabulary helps children with schoolwork because they can spend more time understanding what they're reading and less time decoding the words they're reading.

The path to raising an avid reader—a fifth grader who reads twenty minutes a day outside of school versus the average of five minutes a day—is lots of talking and reading with your children. But among parents whose youngest child is 5 or younger, only 60 percent read with their children every day. It's hard to do if you work full-time or have more than one child, parents report.

One good way to make time? Turn off the TV (see page 150).

Say, "You worked so hard!"

When our kids impress us, our response falls into one of several categories:

1. "You figured that out!" (acknowledgment of a specific effort, strategy, or action)
2. "You're so smart." (praise, which is a statement of our opinion)
3. "Wow!" (non-specific praise)

Which one will most help your child to love learning, relish a challenge, and work harder in school? Number 1, acknowledgment. It matters even when baby is just a year old.

Why some kids persevere

Carol Dweck of Stanford has been studying motivation and perseverance since the 1960s. "Why do some students give up when they encounter difficulty, whereas others who are no more skilled continue to strive and learn?" she wondered in an article in *Scientific American*.

It depends, she discovered, on the students' beliefs about *why* they failed: why they didn't get this math problem right or perform that piano piece well. And whether children are praised or acknowledged has a profound role in creating those beliefs.

Children fall into one of two categories:

- Those with a fixed mindset, who believe their successes are a result of their innate talent or smarts
- Those with a growth mindset, who believe their successes are a result of their hard work

Kids with a fixed mindset believe that "you have a certain amount of intelligence, and you really can't do much to change it." So these children are constantly worried: Am I smart enough? Am I being judged? Will I come up short? They need to prove themselves over and over. Their definition of success is proving that they're smart or talented.

In the fixed mindset, mistakes and failures define you. They reveal your flaws, and those flaws are permanent. So it's too risky to take on a challenge. After a failure, these children have no path to success.

Kids with a growth mindset would agree with the statement: "No matter who you are, you can change your intelligence level." They would say intelligence is something you have to work for; it isn't just given to you. This gives them a willingness to persevere through a challenge. Their definition of success is not proving you're smart, but improving yourself.

In the growth mindset, mistakes and failures don't define you. Instead of "I'm a failure," it's "This idea or strategy failed." There's a path to success, and it's in making more effort.

Guess which child is going to learn more? As you might imagine, either view profoundly affects kids' success as they progress through school and life.

Praise vs. acknowledgment

What creates the fixed-mindset child's need for external approval? Praise.

"Praise is an opinion," says parent coach Sandy Blackard, "which children often rightly hear as an expectation. It's more about the adult than the child."

What creates the growth-mindset child's strong sense of self? Acknowledgment. That is, describing what your child did and naming a strength (see page 176). "Acknowledgment allows you to encourage kids without pressure or expectation because it gives them proof that the strength is already there," Blackard says. "Acknowledgment is all about the child, not about you."

≫

«

How to encourage kids

How can we encourage our kids—but in a way that gives them a strong sense of self rather than a need to seek external approval?

Follow Sandy Blackard's Language of Listening® (see page 176). Say what you see your child doing, saying, feeling, or thinking. Name a strength. "You got the jar open. That's persistent." "You asked if I would like a bite. That's considerate." "You chose your clothes. You know what you like."

The more you can point out a strength, even in a less-than-ideal situation, the more you build up your child.

Ideas for strength words from Blackard:

Doing words

Capable, careful, considerate, cooperative, danger-spotter, dependable, fair, friendly, fun, generous, gentle, goal-oriented, helpful, kind, observant, organized, patient, paying attention, persistent, problem-solver, resourceful, responsible, tidy

Saying words

Assertive, direct, honest, polite, respectful, tactful

Feeling words

Affectionate, bold, brave, caring, compassionate, confident, courageous, empathic, energetic, inspiring, intuitive, joyful, optimistic, powerful, sensitive

Thinking words

Appreciative, aware, clever, contemplative, creative, curious, decisive, determined, insightful, know what you need, know what you want, planner, thoughtful

Two ways to plant a growth mindset

Acknowledge instead of praise

Personally, I find that dropping the opinions and judgments takes effort. Strangers, too, frequently praise my articulate daughter for how smart she is. (My response has morphed from smile with silent cringe to shaping her definition of the term: "Yes, you think about things and make connections and ask lots of questions. You're using your brain!")

We're not alone. About 85 percent of parents with young children Dweck surveyed agreed with this statement: "It is necessary to praise children's ability when they perform well on a task to make them feel that they are smart." Dweck thinks this sentiment might be why most parents, even those who have a growth mindset themselves, tend to give praise.

So repeat after me: acknowledge instead of praise.

What might this look like? Watch a video of acknowledgment in action as my daughter struggles with a task: www.zerotofive.net/bonuses.

Give brain lessons

Teach your child that the brain is like a muscle: the more you use it, the stronger it gets. The way you exercise it is by learning new things: practicing skills, making mistakes, and practicing again. As you learn, neurons form new connections. Existing connections get stronger. Your brain literally changes. So intelligence is not fixed.

It's never too late to rewire the brain. Middle-schoolers and college students with fixed mindsets were able to improve academically when they were taught this lesson. The cool thing is that, in these interventions, only the students were taught these lessons—not the teachers or the parents—so the message doesn't have to be 100% consistent to be powerful.

Acknowledgment	Praise
"You kept trying, and then you got it."	"You're so smart!"
"You figured that out."	"What a big boy!"
"Ooh, lines and swirls. You're proud of your drawing!"	"You're really good at drawing."
"That seemed easy for you; looks like you are ready for something more challenging."	"Wow, you got an A without even studying."
"You did your best. You didn't give up."	"You did it better than anyone else. I'm so proud of you!"
"Look how far you've come. You can do it!"	"With more work, you just might get this right."

DO IT NOW Watch a video of acknowledgment in action at www.zerotofive.net/bonuses.

Kids' mindsets form early

Stanford researcher Carol Dweck gathered up fifth graders, randomly divided them in two groups, and had them work on problems from an IQ test. She then told the first group:

"Wow, that's a really good score. You must be smart at this."

She told the second group:

"Wow, that's a really good score. You must have tried really hard."

She continued to test the kids. Kids whose effort was acknowledged were more likely to take the more challenging task when presented a choice. They were more likely to continue feeling motivated to learn, and to retain their confidence as problems got harder.

Kids praised for their intelligence requested the easier task, lost their confidence as problems got harder, and were much more likely to inflate their test scores when recounting them.

Later, Dweck and her colleagues took the study out of the lab and into the home. Every four months for two years, Stanford and University of Chicago researchers visited fifty-three families and recorded them for ninety minutes as they went about their usual routines. The children were 14 months old at the start of the study.

Researchers then calculated the percentages of types of praise parents used. (Parents were told they were participating in a study of child language development, not praise specifically.)

Five years went by. Then the researchers surveyed the children, now 7 to 8 years old, on their attitudes toward challenges and learning. An example: "How much would you like to do mazes that are very hard so you can learn more about doing mazes?" Children with a growth mindset tended to be more interested in challenges.

Which kids had a growth mindset? Those who had heard more acknowledgment of effort as toddlers.

Teach sign language

Wouldn't it be nice if baby could tell you his needs before he's able to talk? Oh, but he can.

First, you learn a handful of signs relevant to baby. For example, the sign for "milk" looks like squeezing a cow udder. "More" is tapping the tips of all fingers and thumbs together. Then you train baby to sign them, too.

This way, your baby can communicate his needs to you months before he can verbalize them. Or he can help you understand what he's so cutely but indecipherably talking about.

A lot less frustration

As you might imagine, being able to communicate (and be understood) vastly cuts down on baby's crying and whining.

Researchers think signing helps prevent the behavior problems connected with language delays, particularly among children with developmental delays or sensory impairments.

Some parents have heard that learning to sign will delay baby's speech, but there's no evidence to support that notion.

Two ways to teach baby

Friends and I took a baby signing class together. We learned dozens of signs: for foods and animals, "mama" and "papa," "hot" and "cold," "hungry" and "thirsty," "more" and "all done," "play" and "sleep," "hurt" and "where," "please" and "thank you."

It's possible for a baby as young as 6 months old to sign after about six weeks of training. Our babies weren't that quick. Maybe that's because we just made the signs whenever we said the corresponding words—more "something we do for fun" than "training." To teach baby the way researchers do, you'd employ operant-conditioning theory. Fancy. It works like this:

Say it's snack time and you bust out pieces of pear. Give one to baby and make the sign for "pear." Then follow these steps:

1. Hold up another piece of pear and wait five seconds for him to make the sign.
2. If he doesn't, make the sign yourself. Again wait five seconds for him to make the sign.
3. If he doesn't, use his fingers to form the sign. Give him the pear. Make the sign yourself.
4. Repeat. (Researchers do this for a five-minute session several times a day.)

If at any point baby makes the sign himself, he gets the pear and a "Yes! That's right: pear!"

As soon as baby occasionally makes the sign within five seconds, increase the delay to ten seconds. Then twenty seconds. This progressive delay is only for step 1. Step 2 stays at five seconds: once you model the sign, help baby make the sign five seconds later.

I didn't get *that* formal about teaching baby sign language. But my laid-back method, which took closer to four months, still worked. I must say, it was pretty cool when my baby signed for "milk" or "potty" before she could say the words. And I loved being able to direct baby to sign "please" instead of whining "unh! unh! unh!" when she felt the desperate need to pick the blueberries out of my oatmeal.

WHERE TO LEARN SIGNS FOR BABY

- Take a class at your library or community center.
- *Sign with Your Baby*, by researcher Joseph Garcia, is one popular DVD program based on American Sign Language.
- Sign2Me makes a CD of catchy songs called "Li'l Pick Me Up!" that help you remember signs. (My favorites: "More Milk," "Please Change My Diaper," "Sometimes When I Am Hungry," and "I Said 'Oww!'")
- ASL University's "First 100 Signs" are good for baby: lifeprint.com

Go beyond just a few signs for bigger vocabulary, better memory

Several decades of research on sign language point to benefits for children with normal hearing. In multiple studies, kids in preschool, kindergarten, or first grade studied American Sign Language for one academic year. The results are intriguing. They are in line with the benefits of any bilingualism (see next page):

A leap in vocabulary. Kindergartners jumped to the equivalent of a second-grade vocabulary.

Better readers. Kindergartners scored higher on reading placement tests.

Kids remember the words longer. Preschoolers' short-term memory was slightly better.

Kids learn ASL quickly and easily. A language that uses gestures and visuals works well for young children, whose control over their hands and eyes develops faster than control over their voice and speech.

Visual-spatial cognition improves. These are the processes we use in identifying an object visually, pattern matching, making mental representations, and in rotation and orientation—skills an engineer or architect would use.

Kids love it. They're enthusiastic about learning, asking for more signs. (They're also better behaved in the classroom, teachers report, because the kids must pay attention.)

The benefits last. Gains in vocabulary were still evident three years later, even though the kids hadn't taken further ASL lessons.

TRY THIS

- *Start by learning the signs you'll use most with baby; don't dive in to the overwhelming task of learning an entire language.*

- *Sign in as many situations as you're able. Our teacher wanted us to aim for regularly using a dozen signs in the first month.*

- *Combine signs as often as you can: "Eat more pasta?" instead of just "pasta?"*

- *Be patient. It takes seemingly forever for baby to start signing, so it's easy to give up or stress about it.*

- *Watch for baby's personalized version of your signs. (My baby's version of "please" was to put both hands on her belly and swipe them to her sides, rather than circling one hand at her chest.)*

Plan playdates in a second language

Parents who want to raise a bilingual baby find that, despite their best intentions, the job is not so clear-cut.

The most common approaches include "one parent, one language" (mom speaks her native language to baby, and dad does the same) and "home/community" (parents speak one language at home, even if that's not both parents' first language, and baby picks up the second language outside the home).

Both strategies ensure that baby understands a second language. But the child often declines to *speak* the second language. The key?

Reinforce that language beyond the family, says researcher François Grosjean. Get help from babysitters, library story times, community events, immersion preschools—and especially playdates.

That's because, to bother retaining a language, kids need to see a clear use for it. Friends who speak that language present a very good reason.

Social interaction triggers learning

Researcher Patricia Kuhl, at the University of Washington, wondered if 9-month-old babies could learn a language they'd never heard. The babies, whose parents spoke only English, read books and played with Mandarin speakers three times a week, for twenty-five minutes at a time, over four weeks. Then Kuhl used noninvasive imaging technology to assess the babies' brain activity as they heard Mandarin sounds. For at least a month afterward, the babies were as good at picking out the vowel and consonant sounds of Mandarin as babies born in Taiwan.

But only if the babies heard the language from a real-live human being. Presented with TV or an audiotape in Mandarin, babies didn't learn a thing. Beyond age 2, kids are better able to learn from screens (see page 150), though social interaction is still best.

≫

《

Being bilingual benefits baby

Parents often fear that learning multiple languages will delay baby's language skills, but there's no evidence to support that notion. Monolingual and bilingual children both hit language milestones within the expected range, studies show. It's also natural for a bilingual baby to alternate between languages in one sentence. Called "code-switching," it's not a sign of language delay or confusion.

Rather, being bilingual is good for baby's brain. Compared with monolingual babies, bilingual babies

- **stay open to learning longer.** Their brains are still able to detect the contrasting sounds of languages at 10 to 12 months old, past the usual window of 8 to 10 months old.
- **are better at switching mental gears.** When we hear the beginnings of a word, our brains immediately begin guessing at the rest of the word. For bilinguals, both languages are activated each time they hear a word. Constantly switching between languages gives the babies a cognitive
- workout. All that practice improves the brain's ability to monitor its environment and to switch between sets of rules in situations unrelated to language. For example, in one study of bilingual and monolingual 7-month-olds, researchers played a sound that cued the arrival of a puppet, which appeared on one side of a screen. When they heard the sound, both groups of babies soon looked to that spot on the screen in anticipation. Then the puppet began appearing on the other side of the screen. The bilingual babies quickly switched to looking in anticipation at the new location. The monolingual babies didn't.
- **are more creative.** When asked to draw a fantastical flower, bilingual 4- and 5-year-olds drew hybrids like a kite flower, while monolingual kids drew flowers missing petals or leaves.
- **are more accurate and more efficient at tasks testing executive function.** Children were asked to reproduce patterns of colored blocks, repeat a series of numbers out loud, define words, and solve math problems in their heads. The bilingual children were "significantly more successful." These mental puzzles test a suite of skills called executive functions, which allow us to plan and prioritize (see page 116).

One language for you, two for baby?

If you're not bilingual, but hoping to raise a baby who is, one approach is to find a nanny who will speak only that language to baby. If that means *you're* unable to readily communicate with the nanny, translate.google.com comes in handy, along with the occasional translation from a friend. Learn at least a little of the language yourself. (I don't know very much Mandarin, but I'm glad that I know baby's plea for *lán méi* means blueberries.) Then plan those playdates.

There's no good guideline for how much exposure is "enough." For one thing, it's nearly impossible for parents to estimate for a researcher how many minutes of each language their child hears in a day. But clarifying your own goals for baby—fluency, or just exposure—will help guide your approach.

Researchers do know it's best to start early. Up to age 7, children are able to achieve fluency in a second language similar to that of a native speaker. After age 7, the level of fluency one can achieve takes a serious dive. Of course, people do learn languages later in life, but via different brain mechanisms and with a lower level of fluency.

GOOD TO KNOW

Bilingual families say it's harder than they expected to be consistent about speaking only one language to baby. A parent may feel more comfortable talking about work in English and talking about leisure in Spanish, and so switch between the two. If friends are over for dinner and all speaking one language, both parents will speak it. As always, there's theory and then there's practice. You have to do what works for you.

Sleep, eat
& potty

Yes, baby has to be taught how to do everything.
A healthy sense of humor helps.

Guard your sleep

It sounds so simple: just sleep when the baby sleeps!

Well, it's not easy—you have so many things you want to do and no other time to do them—but it's pretty much your only option. Getting a decent amount of sleep might save your job and your marriage, not to mention your sanity.

Sleep deprivation sucks

- Sleep loss hurts a range of cognitive abilities: your ability to regulate strong emotions, to find the right word to communicate, to see someone else's perspective, to hold things in your memory, to react quickly. This starts happening after only two weeks of getting six hours of sleep per night.
- Couples are more often hostile toward each other after baby arrives, making it harder to create an emotionally stable home environment (see page 26).
- Chronic sleep loss and depression are closely related.

Drop everything

The moment baby arrives, let go of checking your e-mail, running your errands, working on your hobbies, watching your TV shows, posting frequently online, and pretty much everything else in your previous life. In the early weeks, focus on feeding your baby, getting sleep, and letting your body heal. Other things can come later. If your partner can't take a leave from work, find a relative or friend who can come stay with you, to focus on caring for you and managing the house while you recover. Yes, you need to be taken care of right now, too.

Go to bed (gasp!) early

No matter how late you stay up, baby is probably going to get up at the same time each morning. So do the math. If baby generally wakes at 6:00 a.m., and is up ninety minutes at night, and you do best on eight hours of sleep, get yourself to bed by 8:30 p.m. "But," you argue, "how will I get this or that done? How will I get any 'me' time?" You won't. Sleep is more important right now.

If possible, stagger bedtimes with your partner and share middle-of-the-night duties. In the morning, baby generally will want to nap ninety minutes after waking, and perhaps you should, too. As needed, have someone—family, friend, neighbor, postpartum doula, babysitter—watch the baby while you catch up on sleep. They say it takes a village. That starts now.

TRY THIS

In the first weeks, go to bed early and don't get up—meaning, don't shower and get dressed and decide you're up for the day—until you've accumulated eight hours of sleep.

Guard baby's sleep, too

Sleep is vital. Well-rested babies are better able to consolidate memory, to focus, and to adapt. They're less easily frustrated, less irritable, and less fussy.

One of the best things you can do right from the start is to not keep baby up too long during the day. New parents inadvertently do this by missing (or ignoring) baby's sleepy signs and keeping baby in an environment that's too stimulating.

Unfortunately, babies don't fall asleep just because they're tired. The biorhythm that governs our wake-sleep cycles only reduces alertness; it doesn't force sleep. So help baby out: create favorable conditions (low light, a bed, a walk) at favorable times (when baby is sleepy).

Find baby's timing

Newborns aren't awake much, but when they are, it shouldn't be for more than forty-five minutes at a time. From 6 weeks to 6 months old, baby wants to stay awake ninety minutes or so (it can vary by thirty minutes in either direction). Then, through 1 year old, the window gradually increases to three hours.

To find your baby's timing, look for sleepy signs: rubbing eyes or ears, staring off into middle distance, becoming less coordinated, or getting more fussy. If you see your baby's signs, help baby sleep. Some babies are good at propping their eyelids open; if so, a meltdown is a sure sign baby needed to sleep.

Awake times lengthen as the brain matures, and as environmental cues (like daylight) and social cues (like your family's daily rhythm) weigh in.

Other tips for timing

Only fools rush in. New parents often come running at baby's first noise during a nap. But starting around 4 months, babies spend the first twenty to forty minutes in "active sleep," before falling into a deeper "quiet sleep" for about sixty minutes. In active sleep, babies might sigh, cry a little, jerk limbs, or even open their eyes. They wake more easily during active sleep. Baby may fall back asleep—or stay asleep—if you just hang back and listen instead of going in to check. If baby falls asleep nursing, or while bouncing with dad, keep it up until baby moves from active to quiet sleep. Then transfer baby into bed. After all that work getting baby to sleep, you *really* don't want her popping awake the second she hits the crib. (Ask me how I know.)

Help baby transition. After one cycle of active sleep plus quiet sleep, baby either wakes or starts another cycle. Some babies easily transition between active and quiet sleep (likely the babies we think of as "good sleepers"). Some don't. If baby wakes up too quickly from a nap, try soothing him back to sleep.

Let go. If helping baby fall asleep for naps is a huge struggle, give up after twenty or thirty minutes. Your timing was just off. I went through this obsessive phase when our daughter was 4 months old, trying for far too long to get naps. It was exhausting. I don't recommend it.

Don't skip naps or push out bedtime. After three months, baby's sleep schedule becomes more organized. Many babies, mine included, want to wake up around 6:00 a.m. no matter what time they went to bed. (Thank goodness my husband does, too.) Don't skip baby's naps, or move bedtime back, trying to get baby to sleep in. All that does is create an overtired baby. It may seem counterintuitive, but for babies, less sleep today doesn't mean more sleep tonight.

GOOD TO KNOW

Infants tend to nap ninety minutes after waking up, even if they just slept all night.

Help baby sleep better at night

Babies take months to regulate their sleep, but you can help give baby the right idea.

Give baby clues about night and day. Newborns sleep (and eat and poop) throughout a twenty-four-hour period. They don't know night from day. Sorry! Baby will need your help with feeding and soothing every couple of hours, as baby focuses on getting enough food into that tiny tummy and regulating internal systems, which used to be regulated by mom's body. This takes about three months. On the plus side, there's no point getting all anxious at this stage about schedules, nap lengths, and whether baby is sleeping through the night.

You can help baby construct his internal clock by exposing him to bright light, noise, and activity during the day, and darkness, quiet, and calm at night.

Sleep in the same room as baby at night. Sleeping near your newborn helps regulate baby's breathing, temperature, and stress levels. It makes breastfeeding easier, because mom and baby's light and deep sleep rhythms sync up. Plus, in the beginning, you're going to constantly check that baby is still alive—might as well do it by opening one eye rather than by getting out of bed.

Probably the easiest way to sleep near baby is a co-sleeper, which is a three-sided crib placed flush against your bed, with both mattresses at about the same level. Co-sleeping is simpler than sharing a bed, which in the West requires some dramatic modifications to be safe.

Bed-sharing requires a firm mattress on the floor by itself, away from walls and furniture that could trap baby, with no loose sheets, blankets, or pillows that could smother baby. Only the mother, who must be sober and a nonsmoker, shares the bed with baby. Bed-sharing means more frequent wakings for both mom and baby, but it may feel right for you. Or it may be the only way baby will sleep. New moms tend to readily fall back asleep after waking; thank you, hormones. But consider transitioning baby to her own bed after a few months. Bed-sharing interrupts and shortens baby's quiet-sleep phase, studies show.

There are other options for beds, given that, after the coziness of the womb, most newborns don't love to lay flat on a huge mattress. Some parents use a baby swing. Legendary Seattle doula Penny Simkin likes the Fisher-Price Rock 'n Play. Both have an inclined back and sloped sides, which make baby feel cozy. The incline also can help if baby has reflux. The Rock 'n Play is small enough to fit next to your bed, and it's lightweight enough to pull around—great for containing baby in a visible place while you do things like shower and eat. Before six months, you transition baby to a crib.

Having baby in your room for a few months means giving up some privacy as a couple, but (if you're getting enough sleep to care) you can find that in other ways.

Swaddle for better sleep. A swaddling blanket or strap snugly wraps baby's arms straight against his sides. This helps baby sleep longer; without it, his arms randomly startle during sleep, potentially waking him up. Swaddling also makes baby more comfortable with sleeping on his back. Newborns must be put to sleep on their backs to reduce the risk of sudden infant death syndrome, or SIDS.

Newborns often protest swaddling at first, because in the womb they're used to having their hands near their mouths. So you might think, "My baby hates this thing; forget it." Not so fast! Finish swaddling, and then immediately comfort baby: nurse, or walk while patting the bum and shhh-shhh-shhh-ing. (This was my doula's tip for introducing baby to slings, wraps, or buckle carriers, too.)

≫

«

Some babies (and parents) fuss at one type of swaddle but like another. Options:

- **Velcro designs** are easy for you to get on, but easy for some babies to get off.
- **A large, thin blanket.** This is the most versatile option. You can swaddle baby arms bent or straight; you can create a divot between the legs if baby will be strapped into a seat. They double as regular blankets and spit-up cloths. Most receiving blankets are too small or bulky; look for muslin.
- **A double swaddle.** This involves using a second blanket or a fabric strap to secure baby's arms inside a traditional swaddle. (Look it up to see a video.) There are premade ones, too. No way baby can bust out of that thing.

Whichever blanket you choose, your swaddling technique must allow baby to move his hips, to prevent hip dysplasia, and to take a deep breath. The arms are what must be snug. Practice on a doll—or sleeping baby, if you dare—to get the hang of it.

Will every single baby on Earth go for being swaddled? Nope. Don't give up on the first try, but trust your intuition about *your* baby.

Create a bedtime routine. Sometime after baby settles into a discernable sleep pattern, around 4 months old, do the same few things in the same order at the same time, every night before bed. Maybe it's a massage, pajamas, and a song. This creates predictability for baby and signals it's time to wind down. After three weeks of a consistent routine, moms in one study reported that babies were falling asleep more quickly, staying asleep longer, and waking up fewer times during the night. Moms' moods improved, too.

Make bedtime daddy time. After six months, baby no longer *needs* food during the night. So, to help set baby's internal clock, encourage baby to feed more during the day by gradually reducing nursing time or bottle amounts at night. If baby wakes up, dad can go in for one minute to soothe. Keep the soothing quiet, low-key, and in the dark. It also often takes far less time for dad to put baby to bed at night than for mom. Something about the lack of breasts . . .

Use a sound machine. Continuous sound can help baby transition between sleep cycles. (Not to mention you . . . especially if someone snores.) Get a machine with options. A low-pitched sound is more soothing than a high-pitched sound.

Around 6 months old, move up bedtime. As soon as baby drops the third nap, move up bedtime. Otherwise, baby won't get enough sleep overnight. My husband and I had to play around with this to find the right time. We put baby to bed fifteen or thirty minutes earlier each night, so long as she continued to wake for the day at 6:00 a.m. If she woke up earlier than usual or took longer to fall asleep than usual, we knew the bedtime was too early. We settled on a bedtime between 6:30 and 7:00 p.m., which was awesome for getting some time to ourselves in the evenings.

Get outside. Babies who slept better at night were exposed to significantly more blue-spectrum light between noon and 4 p.m.

Get help. Solid resources include sleeplady.com, happiestbaby.com, and preciouslittlesleep.com. See which one fits you best.

> **GOOD TO KNOW**
>
> By 4 months old, 85 percent of babies sleep for at least a five-hour stretch, a study using time-lapse video showed. But 15 percent don't. By 1 year old, 73 percent of babies sleep between 10:00 p.m. and 6:00 a.m. But 27 percent don't. On top of that, all babies go through developmental phases that interrupt their previous (sterling, or tolerable, or at least predictable) sleep habits.
>
> So, prepare for a long haul. Your expectations surrounding sleep will color whether you view parenting as stressful.

Give baby chances to self-soothe

....

Most babies need help learning how to fall asleep, or fall back to sleep on their own.

I've seen, with my own eyes, babies who just close their eyes and drift off to sleep when you lay them in bed. (OK, one baby.) Our newborn? She cried. Like many parents, we soothed baby all the way to sleep by any means necessary: Nursing, Harvey Karp's Five S's, walking and patting. Then we'd wait until she was in "quiet sleep" (see page 79), lay her down, hold our breath, and tiptoe away.

Are you doing that, too? It's all right. It was necessary. But around six months, start letting baby fall asleep with gradually less attention. Otherwise, you are likely setting yourself up for desperation—and crying it out—later.

Studies show it helps if you

- wait a bit before you respond to awakenings,
- put baby to bed sleepy but not 100 percent asleep, and
- put baby in his own room.

This is scary because it means changing what you know works. Easygoing babies may not mind the change. Others will mind—and let you know about it.

One gentle method is to create a cue for "I'm going to lay you down now." Mine was singing a lullaby three times, then humming it as I laid her down. Walk out. Come back in if baby is crying. Repeat. Another method is "fading" (see page 88). All the back and forth can feel like *this is not working.* But it is. The purpose is giving baby *chances* to self-soothe, letting him practice.

Similarly, if you usually go to baby the moment he cries in the middle of the night, wait a few moments before you go in. See if the cry escalates or not. This gives baby another chance to self-soothe.

Moving baby's bed to a separate room can help because you're not aware of and responding to every night waking. And when baby wakes up, he doesn't think, "Hey, I see you *right there*. How about a little assistance?" But even if you want to keep baby's crib in your room a while longer, get going on those first two bullet points.

Why start this tough process around six months? Because baby has settled from a big developmental leap around four months. After eight months, baby makes another big leap: a fuller understanding of "object permanence." (Though some researchers think this happens at three or four months.)

That means baby can remember whether you were there when she fell asleep. It's disconcerting to her if conditions aren't the same when she wakes up throughout the night. She cries for you to come back and re-create the proper conditions. A pacifier (apt to fall out of baby's mouth), or a sound machine on a timer, can cause the same trouble.

So around six months, you have a relatively stable developmental window to work with. Even if you're not feeling desperate for decent sleep, don't put off supporting baby's ability to self-soothe. If you do, studies hint, baby may begin to lose the ability.

We thought we had the self-soothing thing down. Bedtime seemed easy; baby slept well. But then it came time to transfer baby to a crib. Oh, she screamed at that crib. As soon as we'd lay her down, she'd pull herself up to standing in the crib and wail.

I wished we'd transitioned baby to the crib earlier, when she still fit in her Rock 'n Play bed. Then we could have more gradually introduced her to the crib: letting her play in it each day until she was comfortable; then trying for naps; then trying for overnight sleep. But that was a moot point.

What worked for us was a little extra TLC that supported baby's self-soothing abilities. My husband would hold baby on his shoulder, walking and singing until her body relaxed. He'd lay her down in bed not quite asleep. Then he'd place his hand on her tummy, gently holding her in place, and shhhhh until she relaxed again. Then he'd walk out, still shhhhh-ing.

Still, baby was waking up through the night. With her crib in our room, it was easy for her to request our help falling back asleep. She'd stand up and cry. I practiced with baby during the day on getting back down to the mattress. She got it. But at night, she'd repeatedly squat and reach for the mattress, then change her mind. (Agh, so close!) Desperate, we veered from sleep book to sleep book. We tried laying baby down again and again, hoping she wouldn't bother to stand up again. (This would go on for more than an hour; she'd win.) We tried lying on the floor, patting the crib mattress for so long we'd practically fall asleep. (Is that being consistent or just stupid?)

After two months of nightly struggles, at 9 months old, we gave up. We moved baby to her own room to cry it out. We gave her a tour of her new surroundings and told her if she needed to cry a little, it was OK, but we'd open the door in the morning. We braced ourselves for rounds of heartbreaking crying.

Not one peep! She instantly slept through the night. It almost seemed like *we'd* been the ones keeping *her* up.

Eighty babies were videotaped sleeping at 1, 3, 6, 9, and 12 months old. The study was led by Melissa Burnham and Thomas Anders at the University of California–Davis. As you might expect, most of the babies became better at self-soothing over time, as they matured. But 40 percent became worse at self-soothing over time. The babies who lost their self-soothing abilities tended to be put to bed after they were already asleep. They slept in their parents' rooms, and they didn't have a "lovie" to cuddle.

Crying it out, a certain way, is OK

If you're utterly exhausted from sleep deprivation, you may begin to ask: When will this baby sleep through the $@%! night? And how do I make that happen right $@%! now?

You may begin to read every single book and blog post in existence about how to get your baby to sleep through the night. And your head may begin to spin.

One of the most controversial methods of sleep training is leaving baby alone for a few minutes at a time to cry herself to sleep. Battle lines are drawn between those who are certain it will scar baby for life and those who swear it's the only thing that worked to get everyone a full night's sleep.

A long-term study says baby will be fine. That is, if babies are at least 8 months old, and parents do not leave them to cry indefinitely.Researchers from Australia and the UK, led by Anna Price, studied several hundred babies 8 months old. (You shouldn't try sleep training, it's generally agreed, before 6 months old.)

Two versions of crying it out:

Controlled crying
You briefly—as in, less than a minute—comfort baby with a back rub and some gentle words that she probably can't hear through her crying, then leave the room and close the door for three minutes. Repeat, staying away for five minutes. Then ten minutes. Cap it at ten. Incrementally, over a week, increase baby's time alone. (See the schedule in *Solve Your Child's Sleep Problems* by Richard Ferber.)

Camping out/fading
You sit near baby's bed and try to soothe with your voice, such as singing a song, until baby is asleep. Each night over three weeks, you move your chair incrementally farther away, until it's out the door.

The study did not look at leaving baby to cry indefinitely. Researchers don't endorse it because of the toxic effects of unrelenting stress (see page 16).

More sleep, less depression

Parents chose which method to use; some tried both. A control group tried neither. Short term, crying it out helped. At 10 months old, 56 percent of babies who cried it out had sleep problems, while 68 percent of controls had sleep problems. At 12 months old, it was 39 percent vs. 55 percent. After two years, fewer mothers were depressed: 15 percent vs. 26 percent.

At six years, the researchers followed up again. Were the kids who had cried it out as infants more stressed than the kids in the control group? How did their mental health, social skills, sleep problems, and relationship with their parents compare? What about the mother's depression, anxiety, and stress (which are linked to infant sleep)?

On every count: no difference.

This study doesn't say parents *should* let baby cry it out. The study says only that, if you want to try controlled crying or camping out, it can reduce sleep problems while doing no harm at this age.

Before you go

Crying it out is not the first place to start. Make sure you've tried the other strategies in this section. If you decide to do it, you must commit to consistency. Giving in randomly will cause baby to cling even more tightly to crying. Then, give it a week. This is hard because you want immediate results, and every day feels like a week. Plus, decisions made groggily at 2:00 a.m. aren't always the ones you intended. Take notes on what you're really doing at each night waking, so you can tell whether you're on your intended path—or just think you are.

Just when you think you've got bedtime figured out, something will change.

My husband and I struggled through this when our 22-month-old figured out how to open her bedroom door after we'd put her to bed. That meant a bleary-eyed baby was stumbling into the living room, making random requests: "Hungry. [Insert food she'd declined to eat at dinner]. Milk! I want to sleep with Mommy and Daddy. Listen to music? Ride my bicycle! I want to walk outside."

Naps were not happening; she wasn't sleeping through the night anymore. Round and round we'd go, baby repeatedly popping out of her room moments after we put her there. We tried various responses—gently returning her to bed again and again, more food, a stint on the potty, ignoring her, counting to three, holding the door closed—until I'd had it and would yell, "Get back in your bed!" and firmly dump her there. Which didn't work, either.

Finally, we started laying down on the floor next to baby's bed until she fell asleep. We were relieved to have found *something* that worked. But it was also disruptive to our own sleep, and it wasn't teaching her how to stay in bed on her own. We needed to step back and think. It was obvious that baby didn't need any of the food or toys she was requesting, and our attention just reinforced her behavior. We needed to stop providing that kind of attention. Maybe she didn't have the self-control to stay in her room now that she had gained the ability to get out. We decided to remove the option of opening the door. Maybe our bedtime routine—laying her down with a bottle and kissing her head—was too short, and bed felt like a place where she got left behind while we continued our evening.

New plan: we put a lock on the door (with baby's help). I let her test the handle to feel the difference between locked and unlocked. I told her she wouldn't be able to open the door when it was locked, and this would help her stay in her room at night. We would open the door in the morning.

We changed our bedtime routine, reading baby three stories as she lay in bed. My husband snuggled in close, so she'd get more cuddle time. Then we said good night. Baby immediately climbed out of bed. This time, we did our own version of "fading": we sat outside the door, instead of laying on her floor, to comfort her.

"I want Mommy to lay on the floor," she cried at the door. "Sad baby!"

"Aww, sad baby," I replied. "Yes, Mommy is right here on the floor. When we're sleepy, we lay down. You can lay on the floor or climb into bed." She wandered back to bed. We repeated this a few times. "I'm going to sing you a song, sweetie, to help you stay in bed," I said.

My song calmed her crying for a bit. When she cried again, I sang again. If she said, "I want Mommy to lay on the floor," I repeated, "Yes, I'm right here on the floor. I'll sing you a song."

This lasted for half an hour as she wandered between the door and her bed, crying off and on. "Get me OUT of here!" she said at one point. I tried not to laugh. I sang to her probably a half-dozen times as she woke up throughout the night. Each instance took less and less singing to calm her. The next night, she stayed in bed from 7:30 p.m. to 6:30 a.m.—the usual. A week passed. Bedtime was back on track.

I tell such a detailed story to make a few points. First, to solve the problem, we couldn't just be indignant that baby wasn't following our orders (although we were). We had to take a step back and try to figure out why baby might be doing this. Locking the door wasn't enough; I tried that for a couple of naps and was met with screeching. We also had to address what we guessed was baby's desire to spend more time with us or her sudden dislike of being left in bed. (Looking back, if we had started there, we could have avoided the lock—see next page.)

Second, be willing to back out of an unsustainable solution, like laying on the floor was for us, and start over.

Third, give your new and improved plan a chance. Once we decided on our plan of empathizing and comforting from outside the door, we had to use it many times throughout the night. If we'd said after the first fifteen minutes, or after the first middle-of-the-night wakeup, "Well, she's still not staying in bed; that didn't work," we would have given up too soon.

Finally, you can see that baby is getting emotional support even though fading is a "cry it out" technique.

Say "Excuse me" to keep kids in bed

Somewhere around age 3, my friends and I are finding, our good sleepers suddenly aren't.

They want us in the room until they fall asleep. They want to climb into our beds in the middle of the night. (Actually, we find this sweet.) Or they refuse to even start the night in their own beds. (Less sweet.) My kid stays in bed for a story but then immediately jumps out of bed with a sly smile. Thus begins a frustrating routine of coming out of her room a dozen times, instead of lying in bed and relaxing.

Most sleep advice for kids revolves around the concept of "extinction": ignoring behavior you don't want. Whether it's extinction (Weissbluth), graduated extinction (Ferber), or graduated extinction with parental presence (everyone else), parents are often missing one key ingredient, says pediatric psychologist Brett Kuhn. Extinction doesn't teach your child what she should be doing.

Kuhn combines extinction with skill-building through positive reinforcement. He calls this the "Excuse Me Drill":

Roll up your sleeves the first night: this will be a full-time job. Delay bedtime a little bit so your child is definitely sleepy.

Sit next to your child in bed and give lots of touch—massage, scratching his back, rubbing his earlobes.

Say, "You're doing a great job staying in bed. Excuse me, but I need to go do something. I'll be right back." Leave and come back right away.

Resume the touch. Describe anything positive you see: "Wow, look at you. You're lying in bed. Your legs are relaxed. Excuse me, I'll be right back." Leave and come back.

Repeat. This is called "thick schedule reinforcement." Using your presence, you're frequently reinforcing the behavior of staying in bed and relaxing.

If your child is doing well, start coming back in intermittently. The timing needs to be unpredictable. As any casino knows, unpredictability encourages a person to keep trying (staying in bed) for the reward (you). You might be doing this twenty times the first night.

Make sure you're not in the room at the moment your child falls asleep. Otherwise he's missing the whole point: initiating sleep on his own.

"Thin" the reinforcement schedule based on how your child is doing. You might do this half as many times on the second night, for example.

Keep thinning, night after night, until it's no longer needed at all.

TRY THIS

At some point, usually between age 3 and 5, your child will no longer need a daily nap. You'll know because your child really fights it, or taking a nap suddenly pushes bedtime way back. The transition sucks: it's bad news if he naps and it's bad news if he doesn't. You'll have to experiment here. (You're used to that, right?) For us, "dropping the nap" actually meant "seriously needs to nap two or three times a week and will do so only in motion." Just when I was about to sell the jogging stroller, I found myself scheduling naps in it. Whatever happens, hang on to that time each day. Make it quiet time instead.

DO IT NOW If your child (age 2+) is waking up too early, I've got a strategy for you at www.zerotofive.net/bonuses.

Make bedtime less crazy

Older kids hear "Time for bed! Brush your teeth!" and somehow—is this universal?—it gets translated into "Run!"

So you're chasing them every step of the way. A routine chart halts the chase by creating very clear, consistent rules for bedtime.

Create a visual chart

The secret to an effective routine chart is to create it together with your kids. Your children gain some control over the process, and they're more enthusiastic about following a plan they've helped create. As kids get used to following the chart, which can take several weeks, hassles and power struggles begin to vanish.

1. **Brainstorm a list of the steps.** Sit down with your kids and ask them to tell you everything they need to get ready for bed. Take notes. Narrow it down to seven items or less (maybe only three for little kids, like "bath, jammies, story").

2. **Have your children illustrate each task.** They can draw pictures, or you can take pictures of them doing the task. Together, paste the pictures, in order, onto a poster. The chart doesn't need to have words or checkboxes. It doesn't need places for stickers; bribes and rewards create only short-term motivation. Make just a row or two of pictures that will remind your kids what to do next.

3. **Spend time on success training.** Focus on practicing one step per night, giving a little tutorial on each step. Return to the chart as soon as one task is done. Be the cheerleader instead of the police, says parent coach Sandy Blackard: "Lights out is at 8:00 p.m. Cuddling and story time starts when bath, jammies, and teeth are done. You can have long, short, or no cuddling/story time. Which do you want tonight? Long, OK. Show me how quick you can get ready."

4. **Let the routine chart be the boss.** When the kids get off task (intentionally or not): "What's next so that we can get to story time?" "As soon as ___, then ___." Point out successes and give reminders: "You did ___ and ___ already. There's another step!" For kids younger than 5, do the tasks along with them.

If your child still resists? Calmly point, lead, or carry him to the chart, and ask again. Or remind him that story time is coming once he brushes his teeth. Or say, "I'll be in your bedroom. Come find me when you're ready to put on your pajamas."

TRY THIS

Make bedtime more crazy!

The Natkin family found that evenings went more smoothly when they added five minutes for everyone to get crazy together—dance party! tickle fest!—before settling down for bed.

If bedtime is still a constant struggle after using your routine chart, parent coach Sarina Natkin says, ask yourself what piece is missing. Do the kids need more time with you? More control over the process?

If your child is constantly popping out of bed with requests, add those items to your routine: "Let's make sure you have everything you need before bed." Or try "bedtime tickets": kids can use two tickets per night to make requests. Any additional request is ignored, and the child is gently but silently deposited back in bed.

Whenever a plan isn't working, kick it back to your family meeting (see page 144) so that you can brainstorm solutions.

Be laid-back about breastfeeding

Like the rest of parenting, breastfeeding is both rewarding and hard work. A relaxed attitude goes a long way.

Sixty percent of women want to breastfeed exclusively. But two-thirds of those women give up, studies show. Why? Women cited breastfeeding pain, worry that they weren't producing enough milk, and problems getting baby to latch. Expect that you'll experience these common issues, too. But trust that the right support can help you through.

Comfort is key

The first thing to know is: get comfortable. If you're not comfortable, adjust your body or baby's body. If your nipples are killing you, unlatch baby and try again. Breastfeeding your baby isn't supposed to cause searing pain in your neck, wrists, or nipples—at least not for long.

Start with the laid-back breastfeeding position. (One lactation consultant joked that if everyone used this technique, it would put her out of business.) Sit down, then scoot your hips forward and lean back, like you're slouching to watch TV. Place baby on her tummy against your chest, at any angle that's comfortable, and let her find your breast. It's easier for everything to fall into place than if you're sitting upright or lying down. Plus, you're supporting baby's body with your body instead of tiring out your arms. See biologicalnurturing.com for videos and more information.

Feed a calm baby

Practice when baby is calm rather than crying. It's easier for her to learn, and her tongue will be in the right place. Try to catch her hunger signs (rooting, hand to mouth) before she gets really upset. If she's upset, calm her first before you feed her.

Milk out = milk in

The more breast milk baby removes, the more breast milk you produce. So if your doctors tell you that baby needs formula, but you want to preserve the option of breastfeeding, you need to start pumping immediately. Work up to pumping at the highest setting you can stand, because (when things are working properly) babies remove more milk than pumps can.

Get support

Talk with your doctor. Your hospital might get you off to a good start. International guidelines are to initiate breastfeeding within the first hour after birth; place baby and mom together 24-7; encourage breastfeeding on demand, not on a schedule; and don't provide formula unless medically necessary. You can make these requests. Some hospitals and community centers offer breastfeeding support groups as well.

Line up help. New moms need care just as baby does. But in the US, women tend to expect themselves to quickly get back to cleaning, cooking, and exercising. Resist. Good websites: kellymom.com, llli.org, ilca.org.

THE RESEARCH

Breast is brainiest . . . by a little bit

Each month of breastfeeding adds a small gain, about one-third of a point, to your child's intelligence scores. Researchers from Harvard and Boston Children's Hospital studied data on more than thirteen hundred mothers and children. They adjusted for a host of factors, including socioeconomic status, the mother's intelligence, and whether baby was raised at home or in day care. The longer baby breastfeeds, they found, the higher baby's vocabulary scores at 3 years old and intelligence scores at 7 years old. A baby breastfed for twelve months would score four IQ points higher than a baby who was not breastfed. IQ does matter. But if breastfeeding just isn't working, there are plenty of other ways to help fulfill baby's intellectual potential.

GOOD TO KNOW

Breast milk isn't just food. Your body responds to baby's needs day to day by adjusting hormones, immune factors, volume of milk, sugars to feed the bacteria in baby's gut, and surely more properties that researchers haven't discovered yet.

"Eat food. Not too much. Mostly plants."

"My kid eats what I eat," you hear parents say, happy they're not preparing separate meals for their child.

For me, the reverse has turned out to be true. I found myself being so careful about feeding my baby healthy food, I realized *I* should eat more of what *baby* was eating.

Case in point: baby drinks a kale smoothie most days, an easy way to get her greens. (It tastes better than it sounds.)

Easier said than done

Food journalist Michael Pollan's advice—the title of this page—is based on the way humans ate for hundreds of thousands of years. Grasses, fruits, vegetables, small mammals, insects, and a distinct lack of sugar—this is the diet our brains and bodies function best on.

I've been working toward eating this way for fifteen years and counting. (Well, except for the insects.) If you're trying to do that, too, here are the things that have made it easier for me post-baby:

Buying fresh, local produce. Great-tasting food starts with high-quality ingredients. I'd heard that but didn't really know what it meant until I took a cooking class. We sampled organic carrots shipped to a big supermarket (dull, dense, bitter) and organic carrots freshly picked from a local farm (crisp, lively, sweet). The difference was a revelation.

Living in Seattle, I'm fortunate to have a farmers' market within walking distance and several options for community-supported agriculture programs. In a CSA program, you "subscribe" to a local farm each season in exchange for a box of produce delivered regularly. Our weekly box of produce is full of variety I never would have thought to buy on my own—delicata squash, eggplants, collard greens, kale, cabbage, sunchokes, beets.

Produce straight from the farm tastes *good*, even when you do very little to it.

A pressure cooker. I swear this thing should be issued to all new parents at the hospital. You can cook soups, barley risottos, beans, and curries in ten minutes instead of thirty to sixty minutes. These are mainly the meals we eat now.

A powerful blender. A high-end blender makes everything from smooth kale smoothies to broccoli pesto.

Cooking in big batches once or twice a week. Cooking is not a hobby for me. I don't want to do it for every meal. So I aspire to make steel-cut oats, quinoa, roasted vegetables, and hearty soups to last the week. I may wash and chop ingredients one day and cook them the next.

Storing produce properly as soon as I bring it home. I admit, at times we've shoved our whole box of CSA produce into the fridge and promptly gone out for Thai food. My cooking plan works better when I put each item in plain view, so it gets used. And when I store each item properly, so it lasts longer.

>>

«

Simple recipes. My criteria for a recipe: Does it have a minimal number of ingredients? Can I prep the ingredients one day and cook them the next? Will this freeze well if I triple the batch? Now we're talking.

I still can't get over how delicious and easy potato-leek soup is. You just cook four sliced leeks in a little butter until they're soft, add four cups of potato chunks and four cups of broth to the pot, keep cooking until the potatoes are tender, and then briefly blend the soup into a puree. That's four ingredients.

Make it taste good. Cook with fats, spices, and herbs. When we take pleasure in what we're eating, one study found, we absorb more of the nutrients from it.

So far, I've found great recipes at cookusinterruptus.com, nourishingmeals.com, and 101cookbooks.com. I credit smittenkitchen.com for building my confidence with recipes that just plain work.

Backups. I keep a Costco-sized box of Amy's lentil soup in the pantry for when I haven't had time to cook and it's "that kind of day." I also keep Lärabars, which have only a few ingredients, for snacks.

A kale smoothie every day. This is a great way to get raw greens. The fruit masks their taste, so "green juice," as baby calls it, goes down easy. Here's the recipe, adapted from nourishingmeals.com:

> 2 pieces of fruit (apple + pear, peach, or nectarine)
> 2 bunches of greens, thick ribs removed (kale or chard + spinach or collard greens)
> 1/2 cup of cabbage, chopped
> 2 cups of water
> 1 lemon, juiced

Pulse the blender to chop everything, and puree until smooth. If it tastes too sweet, add more greens. If it tastes too green, add more fruit.

- dried fruit, apple pieces, and walnuts
- fruit: berries (bought in bulk and frozen), bananas, grapes cut in half, or a mandarin orange
- pieces of broccoli, cauliflower, and carrots tossed in the microwave for two minutes, maybe with chunks of apple or yams. Or sweet potato, pear, and broccoli. Toss with a tiny bit of coconut oil or avocado oil for fat and a different flavor.
- cherry tomatoes cut in half (Sungold, if you can get 'em), pieces of cucumber, and frozen corn
- avocado chunks: let baby tap a little salt and pepper, or squeeze a lemon, on top

GOOD TO KNOW

Don't worry if baby is a fruit fiend. Just stick to whole fruit. Nature pairs fiber with sugar, so sugar from whole fruit doesn't have the same harmful effect as refined sugar. Look for dried fruit without added sugar. Skip fruit juice—it's missing the fiber.

Let baby decide how much to eat

Imagine if someone hovered over, prodded, and cheered on your every bite: annoying!

Trust baby's signals. Our job as parents is to put a variety of nutritious foods in front of our kids. We're in charge of what, when, and where they eat. It's our kids' job to decide whether they eat and how much they eat.

The goal here is to trust children's internal regulation of consumption, which naturally varies day to day. If we continually override kids' signals with our own (well-intentioned) desires, forcing kids to eat the amount of food we think they should eat, they learn to ignore their body's signals for being hungry or full. That sets them up for an unhealthy relationship with food.

We ask baby, "All done?" I'm still trying to get my husband to accept baby's "Yes" instead of responding with, "Are you sure? All done? Here, take one more bite."

Sit down and eat with your child, at regular times. Family meals have more variety and more nutritious foods, studies show, than you get from skipping meals and grazing. (Many of us have the unfortunate view that meals are a duty and snacks are for enjoyment.) If kids ask for food in between their meal and snack times, offer them water. Bonus: regular meal and snack times make for easier naps, as the body gets used to the rhythm of the day.

With new foods, focus on exposure. Encourage baby to touch and smell a new food, watch you eat it, and perhaps put it in her mouth before taking it out again. Think of this not as baby rejecting the food, but as baby preparing to eventually eat the food.

Introduce a new food many more times than you'd think. Children are often skeptical of new foods, and our expectations are way off about how long it takes for them to acclimate. Exposing kids to a new food eight times over two weeks wouldn't be too much. Keep offering variety, but also make sure baby has a familiar food to fill up on.

Don't plead or command over and over. "Take a bite. Just one bite. Come on, eat your food." Studies show that a high rate of verbal pressure leads kids to refuse food.

Bargain sparingly. Rewards and bargaining do work to jump-start exposure to new food, but they're not the best long-term strategy. In one study, researchers asked children to taste slices of red pepper. They told one group, "You can eat as much as you like." They told a second group, "If you eat at least one piece, you may choose one of these stickers. You can eat as much as you like." The reward group jumped to try the red pepper. But over time, children in the first group ate more red pepper and liked it more.

TRY THIS

Now that our toddler is copying everything we do, putting food on our plate instead of her plate is a surefire way to interest her in it.

Baby likes to see us eat the food. Sometimes we play "One bite for mommy, one bite for daddy, one bite for baby."

Offer the opportunity to potty

There's no evidence that later is better than earlier when it comes to potty training. Only that being gentle is better than shaming or forcing baby.

Before World War II, parents often forced, scolded, and punished 8-month-olds into using the toilet. This was linked to problems: constipation, holding it, refusing to use the toilet. Pediatrician T. Berry Brazelton championed an effort to change that practice. That's a good thing. But some parents have interpreted it to mean they should tiptoe around potty training until the child tells you she's done with diapers—a period that's getting longer and longer as diaper companies make bigger and bigger diapers. There's no need to wait *that* long.

No matter what age you choose to help baby use a toilet, here are a few ways to be gentle:

Provide the opportunity only. Rather than physically forcing or bribing baby to sit on the potty, see it as simply offering the opportunity. Baby decides whether to go. You still have to make an effort to encourage baby to sit on the potty and stay sitting, but don't get worked up if she doesn't.

My husband and I sit nearby and sing a song, read a book, or blow bubbles to help baby sit long enough. We remind her, "Yeah, it takes a while to poop. We sit, lean forward, and wait." If she starts to run off, we say, "All done with potty?" rather than "No, no, you're not done. Sit back down."

Offer the potty regularly: before and after sleep, before and after outings, and thirty to sixty minutes after meals. Kids come to expect potty times without being nagged.

"Time for potty" is our line. (Asking our toddler, at 22 months old, "Do you need to go potty?" elicits a "No," even if she's standing there in a half crouch.) As we walk in the door from an outing, we remind her of the routine: "What's the first thing we do when we come home? Sit on the potty." We might add, "Do you need help?" or "What song should we sing?"

Stay low-key. When baby says, "I need to go potty," if we casually respond, "OK, go for it," she will. If we hover or give too much instruction, she'll change her mind. Afterward, if we say, "Good job going potty," she smiles in satisfaction. If we make a big deal, clapping and exclaiming, then the next time she pees, she'll empty her potty in the toilet, then bring it over to us for praise. (Yikes!)

Go diaper-free. My favorite description of potty training is: "You just take off the diaper." You can go diaper-free at pretty much any age, for any amount of time during the day. As early as a few months old, some parents whisk a jar or tiny pot under baby's bum—or hold baby in a squat position over the toilet—between diaper changes. Other parents sit baby on a potty chair when they use the bathroom. Others try to catch every pee and poo, offering a potty every thirty or sixty minutes. Yes, that's how often many infants need to pee. If baby goes, the parents make a noise: "tsss" or "unh, unh." The cue eventually signals baby to go potty, and it gives baby a way to tell you that she needs to go.

We went diaper-free, at home only, around 12 months old. This was hit and miss—meaning, carpet cleaner came in handy. As soon as baby started running to her potty chair on her own, I just expected that she would every time. But she'd get distracted while playing. So would I. In hindsight, I could have more consistently offered her the potty, plus gotten her sitters on the same page.

Save bedtime for last. Most kids wear a diaper to bed at night until age 4 or 5. Medically, the term "bed-wetting" doesn't even apply to kids younger than 5.

GOOD TO KNOW

Potty training doesn't require complete bladder and bowel control, only an ability to briefly delay the action. Indeed, only 20 percent of children have complete bladder and bowel control by age 2, when many parents start potty training.

If you're waiting to potty train, don't put it off past 32 months. Baby might be at higher risk of urinary tract infections, from not completely emptying the bladder. There's also a higher risk of weak bladder control, which leads to more accidents.

Play

Kids learn an incredibly important skill from playing with their peers: self-control. Before that, though, you're baby's favorite toy: baby loves pulling your hair, pinching your nose, stepping up the front of your body, and going for a ride.

Let baby touch that

It's hard to beat having a variety of direct, hands-on experiences.

You don't have to buy a mountain of stuff to introduce baby to new stimuli:

- While you're cooking or grocery shopping, let baby touch the papery onion skin and the rough avocado peel.
- In your closet, introduce baby to the cashmere sweater and leather pants you never wear anymore.
- On a walk, when you stop to smell the roses, brush a petal against baby's skin. (Wait until baby is 8 months old, when very light touch feels OK.)
- On our walks, my toddler wants to play hide-and-seek by peeking through the slots of Dumpsters. She wants to touch recycling bins. I've come to terms with this. We can always wash hands afterward.
- Store most of baby's toys and regularly rotate them out.
- Trade toys with friends.

Mmm, rocks

Sensitivity to touch develops in the body from top to bottom, starting with the mouth. That's why babies use their mouths to explore objects. (Rocks were particularly compelling for mine.) If a 1-month-old baby is allowed to mouth an object, but not see it, that baby later can recognize the object visually.

Touch sensitivity takes time to spread down the body: the face is more sensitive than the hands even at age 5.

MONEY-SAVING TIP

Baby's favorite toys are whichever things you didn't buy for baby:

- remote control
- keys, wallet, cell phone
- pocket mirror
- calculator
- your shoes: putting their feet in them
- your underwear: wearing it around their neck
- the box the toy came in
- fruit: taking one bite of each and putting it back in the bowl
- laundry basket: going for a spin
- drawers and cabinets: perfect for hiding your keys, wallet, cell phone

Save the box

Which toys are best for baby's brain?
Toys that require baby to *use* his brain.

The best toys don't beep, talk, dance, or flash to hold a child's attention. They require imagination to come alive.

But toy manufacturers know that if they say their products boost baby's development—claims that are rarely scientifically tested—you're more likely to buy them. For example, I was given some soft fabric rattles that fasten around baby's wrist. The package says they develop "sound location skills." Really?

Instead, go for basic toys, like these:

- jars with screw-on lids, bowls and cups of various sizes, and something baby can move from one cup to the other (water, dirt, dried beans)
- couch cushions and pillows, set up as an obstacle course for crawling or climbing
- balls and blocks (Lego Duplo, K'Nex sets, Tegu magnetic blocks, Keva Contraptions, Tinkertoys)
- old-fashioned dolls, finger puppets
- chairs and a blanket, for making a fort
- appliance box and markers, for making a car or spaceship
- tape

Don't forget, *you're* baby's favorite toy. Baby loves to climb on you, be twirled, swung, and tossed by you, squeal at the tickle monster—and sit on the floor with you, playing with these toys together.

GOOD TO KNOW

Playing with blocks improves spatial skills, math skills, problem-solving skills, and cooperation. Playing with dolls helps baby practice social and emotional skills.

Make music with baby

Children encourage you to publicly embarrass yourself in all sorts of ways you didn't imagine.

My baby and I were out for a walk along a wooded path, and a song popped into my head. As I helped baby touch various parts of the nearest tree, I sang, "And on that twig / there was a leaf / the prettiest leaf / that you ever did see!" Thank you, Toddler Radio on Pandora.

I can barely carry a tune. Good thing infants prefer their parents' voices over other voices, and prefer singing directed to them over other kinds of singing.

We sing at home, too, as I pick out "Twinkle, Twinkle, Little Star" on my baby's xylophone. (Hey, three years of piano lessons didn't go to waste after all!)

And we take a parent-tot music class, because baby gets a taste of music as the social experience that it has been for all of human history. She gets to try out instruments we don't have at home. She dances, bounces, picks up rhythm, and tries out tones. And the teacher is so engaging, my baby gives her a hug at the end of class.

Will music lessons make baby smarter?

Musicians are brainier than non-musicians in all sorts of ways. They're better at abstract reasoning, math, reading, vocabulary, fine motor skills, spatial skills, and working memory.

However, researchers haven't been able to prove that music training is the cause. Perhaps parents who are able to afford private music lessons also read more to their kids, for example, and that's what improves their kids' vocabulary and reading skills. Perhaps children with certain cognitive strengths are attracted to music lessons. The half-dozen trials that have sought to establish a cause report mixed results.

But a brain boost was never the best reason to study music anyway.

Music for music's sake

Music is universal: nearly everyone is drawn to it. "Human societies with no music, like human societies with no language, have never been found," Harvard psychologist Roger Brown wrote. Yet no one has to make a case for studying language—the sounds we use to express what's on our minds versus what's in our souls.

In a piece titled "Why teach music?" Kathryn B. Hull, a nationally certified music teacher, wrote of the many aspects of music:

Music is science. It is "exact and specific." A conductor's score is "a graph which indicates frequencies, intensities, volume changes, melody, and harmony all at once and with precise control of time."

Music is mathematical. It's rhythmically based on fractions of time, "often in multiple combinations simultaneously."

Music is a foreign language. "Most of the terms are in Italian, German, or French; and the notation . . . uses symbols to represent ideas. The semantics of music is the most complete and universal language. It speaks to the soul."

Music is history. It "reflects the environment and times of its creation" and "keeps a people's culture alive."

Music is physical education. "It requires fantastic coordination of fingers, hands, arms, feet, lips, cheeks," along with extraordinary muscle control.

≫

DO IT NOW

Keep a variety of musical instruments in baby's toy bin, and jam together. Libraries and children's museums often offer a free weekly music class. Your local symphony may have a children's program, too. The national research-based programs Music Together and Kindermusik both send you home from class with a CD of the songs you learn.

≪

Music is art. What we create and derive from it is "humanism, emotion, feeling—call it what you will."

Hull goes on:

> ### This is why we teach music!
>
> > Not because we expect you to major in music
> > Not because we expect you to play or sing music all your life
> > Not only so you can relax and just have fun
>
> ### But
>
> > . . . so you will be human
> > . . . so you will recognize beauty
> > . . . so you will be sensitive
> > . . . so you will be closer to an infinite beyond this world
> > . . . so you will have something to retain for enrichment
> > . . . so you will have more love, more compassion, more gentleness . . .
> > in short, more life!
>
> > Of what value will it be to make a prosperous living unless you
> > know how to live? Music gives lifelong benefits.
>
> ### That is why we teach music!

GOOD TO KNOW

When you listen to music, the brain uses many networks to process rhythm, timbre, and tone. Not only the brain's auditory areas light up, but so do those areas responsible for motor skills, emotions, and creativity.

When kids snatch toys, wait and see

At 18 months old, my toddler and her playmates readily grabbed toys from each other.

Parents almost always stepped in, prying their baby's fingers from the toy, handing it back, and scolding: "She was playing with that." When baby's face crumples in tears, they implore, "We need to share. Can you share?"

Well, no.

In one experiment, children could choose to give food to a partner or not, but would get food either way. At 25 months old, 57 percent decided to share. At 18 months old, only 14 percent decided to share, even though it came at no cost to them.

We want our kids to be able to play nicely with others. But children are capable of altruistic helping only after they've climbed a couple other rungs in this particular developmental ladder.

Cooperation starts early

Notice, though, how cooperative and helpful your toddler is. She tries to feed her favorite food to her playmate. She insists on helping you sweep the floor. We don't have to teach these things. Humans are wired for cooperation (along with competition), say evolutionary anthropologists; it's how our species survived.

It's just that toddlers aren't good at detecting *when* help is needed. That requires an ability to guess someone else's feelings and state of mind. So toddlers understand certain types of help before others.

Instrumental helping: Between 12 and 14 months old, baby begins to help with simple action-based goals, such as looking for or reaching for an item. Around 18 months old, baby's instrumental helping expands to include overcoming obstacles, using tools, and understanding the means to an end.

≫

Empathic helping: Also around 18 months old, baby begins to express concern for and comfort others. Still, emotion-based helping is pretty limited. By 30 months old, baby is more skilled. Baby can infer others' feelings and intentions, without being told explicitly, and sometimes infer someone's needs.

Altruistic helping: Around 30 months old, baby knows what another person needs, but has trouble giving up something of value. As children gain a greater understanding of the sacrifice that altruism requires, around age 3, they are temporarily even *less* willing to share their possessions.

Help me help you

How much information does a child need to figure out that someone needs help? In one study, led by Margarita Svetlova at the University of Pittsburgh, an adult pretended to be cold. A blanket was within reach of the child but not the adult. The adult went through progressively more explicit cues, five to seven seconds each, until the child brought over the blanket.

1. Gestures: Shivering, rubbing and hugging oneself, saying "Brrr."
2. Naming the internal state: "I'm cold."
3. Stating a general need for an object: "I need something to make me warm."
4. Labeling the object needed: "A blanket!"
5. Nonverbal request: Looking at the child, then the blanket, then the child.
6. Less subtle nonverbal request: Gesturing to the blanket.
7. General verbal request: "Can you help me?"
8. Specific verbal request: "Can you bring me the blanket?"

Guess at which point the average 18-month-old figured it out. Step 6. But by 30 months? Step 2. Unless it was the child's own blanket that the child had to share. Then, the 30-month-old resisted until Step 4. So, it's not that an 18-month-old can't help, cooperate, or share. He just needs explicit instructions about someone else's state of mind. Your toddler's peers are unlikely to offer these kinds of instruction—but you can.

TRY THIS

When playmates grab toys:

Do nothing. Kids usually figure it out on their own, if you don't step in and make an enormous deal about the toy. It's good practice for them. Plus, you'll get to point out a strength: "You figured that out on your own." Agree on this approach with the other playdate parents ahead of time.

Make a direct request. "Please wait your turn. You waited. Now it's your turn."
"Your friend is playing with the toy now. You can ask, 'Please?' If she isn't done yet, say 'I can wait.'"
"Your friend would like to play with the toy now. When can she have it—in one count or three? Three? One, two, three. There. She waited, and you shared!"

If one child gets upset, empathize and state the problem.
"You took your friend's toy, and he feels sad. He wants it back. When can he have it—in one count or three?"
"Your friend took the toy, and you feel sad. Two kids who want the same toy. Hmm ... must be something you can do. (Wait for their solution, then name it.) You're taking turns! You like playing together."

(See page 176 for more on Language of Listening®, the framework used here.)

Play at self-control

Self-control is one of the most important skills your child can develop.

As you can imagine, the ability to start or continue doing something you'd rather not do (like your homework), and the ability to stop doing something you want to do (like watching TV), is a powerful force in creating a successful life.

Many, many studies show this to be the case. Leading researcher Adele Diamond summarizes a landmark 2011 study by Terrie Moffitt, who followed a thousand children for thirty-two years:

> Children with worse self-control (less persistence, more impulsivity, and poorer attention regulation) at ages 3–11 tend to have worse health, earn less, and commit more crimes 30 years later than those with better self-control as children, controlling for IQ, gender, social class, and more.

Self-control—also called self-regulation or inhibitory control—is core to a suite of brain processes called executive function. Inhibitory control, working memory, attention, and cognitive flexibility combine to allow problem solving, reasoning, planning, and delaying gratification.

As students, children with more self-control are

- better able to focus on and complete their assignments,
- better able to pay attention and ignore distractions, and
- better able to integrate new material.

Executive function starts to develop during baby's first year of life. But it won't fully mature until your baby is in his or her early 20s. That's a lot of time to practice.

There are plenty of engaging ways to put the "fun" in executive function:

Tell your own stories
Kids love storytelling. You're looking at each other instead of at a book, getting that face-to-face interaction. And the lack of pictures exercises children's ability to pay attention and keep track of details. Children remember more of the characters and plot from storytelling than from book reading, studies show.

If you're not comfortable telling stories, you could start by recounting your day to your infant, and expand your repertoire from there. Baby doesn't care what the story is about! My stories tend to start with "There once was a girl . . . " and involve whatever exotic thing happened yesterday. You can also look for storytelling events at festivals, schools, and bookstores.

Dance, kick, and make music

See if your child enjoys traditional martial arts, dance, or playing a musical instrument—especially with others. All of these require your child to concentrate, pay attention for long stretches, and hold in mind complex sequences: the steps of the dance, the notes of the song.

Diamond says they also provide joy, give a sense of social belonging, develop motor skills, instill pride, and promote self-confidence—all of which support executive-function development.

≫

OTHER WAYS TO BUILD EXECUTIVE FUNCTION

Exercise. This is one of the best ways to build executive function, among other things (see page 12). Less obviously, yoga and Tae Kwon Do (if noncompetitive) also have been shown to improve executive function in kids.

Set challenging goals: At age 3, building a taller block tower, for example; at age 5, building a birdhouse.

Hobbies: Encourage a passion that takes your child's active effort.

Montessori school: Kids in this program tend to have higher levels of executive function and creativity.

Allow mistakes: See page 156.

A second language: See page 71.

Make-believe: See page 124.

Play games

Classic kids' games are great, too. I remember playing several of these as a kid with my parents and sisters. Not only are they a blast, they help build executive function. In one study, preschoolers played such games for thirty minutes twice a week. After eight weeks, the children's self-regulation scores were significantly better, compared with those in the control group. The researchers, led by Megan McClelland at Oregon State University, studied 276 low-income preschoolers.

The key is that the activity becomes progressively more challenging (with games, you might increase the speed, add rules, or reverse the rules) as kids get the hang of it. Music and movement help, too, so kids don't have to sit still for long.

Here are the traits to look for in games that develop executive function:

Games that require inhibiting one's natural reaction

Freeze: Create a playlist that alternates between your favorite slow and fast songs. Everybody dances when you play the music, and everybody freezes when you hit stop. Dance slowly to slow songs and quickly to fast songs—then the opposite.

Color-Matching Freeze: Tape various colors of construction paper to the ground. Follow the rules above, except also hold up a color when the music stops. Everybody has to run and stand on that color paper before freezing.

Conducting an Orchestra: When one person is "conducting," the others play their instruments (bells or pots and pans or whatever you have). When the conductor puts down the baton, the playing stops. Then switch the rule so that the players play quickly when the baton waves quickly, and vice versa. Try opposites: when one person is conducting, the others stop playing, and vice versa.

Games that require paying close attention

Drumbeats: Come up with body movements (like clapping, stomping, walking, or dancing). Match them to drum cues. Kids could walk quickly to fast drumming, walk slowly to slow drumming, and freeze when you stop drumming. Or they could hop to fast drumbeats and crawl to slow drumbeats.

Walk in a Line: Make a game of walking along a line in the sidewalk, the line between planks in a wooden floor, painters' tape you've put across the carpet, or a log on the ground.

Games that require cognitive flexibility

Sleeping, Sleeping, All the Children Are Sleeping: The kids pretend to sleep while you sing, "Sleeping, sleeping, all the children are sleeping." Then make up an animal that the kids have to stand up and act out, saying: "And when they woke up . . . they were monkeys!"

Games that require focusing on one thing while ignoring others

Slug Bug: When kids see a Volkswagen Beetle during a drive, they yell "Slug bug!" Or "Yellow car!" or whatever color/car model/phrase you come up with. They can rack up points instead of punches if you prefer.

Alphabet: Find each letter of the alphabet, in order, on signs and buildings (and, for a faster game, license plates) during a drive.

Games that work on working memory

Clap Your Hands: Cut a big square, circle, and triangle from construction paper. Have one person choose an action for each shape, such as clap your hands (square); stomp your feet (circle); and touch your nose (triangle). The leader holds up or points to the shapes in order (square, circle, triangle, repeat), performing each action to demonstrate. Then the leader indicates the shapes in order as the kids perform the matching action together. Try going faster and faster. Try switching cues so that the kids must also inhibit what they just learned: touch your toes (square); raise your arms (circle); jump (triangle). The leader continues indicating the shapes in order.

I'm Going on Vacation and I'm Bringing . . . The first player lists an item that starts with A. The second player repeats that item and adds one that starts with B. The next player repeats both items and adds one that starts with C, etc.

What executive functions look like

Child

Inhibitory control *ability to resist the urge to do one thing and instead do what is most appropriate*	• resists a smaller reward if given the option of a greater reward in the future • goes to the end of the line instead of cutting • reaches around a glass display instead of trying to reach straight for an item inside
Working memory *ability to hold information in mind and work with it*	• connects a phrase from a song to something seen during a walk • does a math problem in her head
Attention *ability to focus your attention and resist distraction*	• concentrates on building a castle, despite a sibling racing around • looks for mom in the mall, screening out everything else to see only her face
Cognitive flexibility *ability to switch perspectives; ability to adjust to changed demands or priorities*	• changes strategies when action isn't getting the desired result • during make-believe, goes with the flow as characters change

Adult

- stops binge-watching *Breaking Bad*, turning off the TV instead of hitting "Next episode"
- thinks before speaking
- goes for the fruit instead of the cake after resolving to eat more fruit and less cake

- relates something read in a history book to a current political event
- mentally reorders errands based on their distance from the house

- resists posting on social media to complete a project for work
- at a party, concentrates on the conversation at hand, even though many people are speaking

- sees different peoples' points of view, or sees their reasons for saying what they said or wanting what they wanted
- finds an alternate route when the planned route is blocked
- adjusts when things don't go according to plan

THE RESEARCH

Many studies show that preschoolers' and kinder-garteners' executive-function scores are more important than their IQ scores for later academic success. Young children with better executive function

- tend to be more than three months ahead of their peers in early literacy,
- have higher levels of academic achievement from elementary school through college,
- do better on standardized tests, such as the SAT,
- tend to have positive relationships with peers and teachers (they're less disruptive, inconsiderate, or aggressive, which in turn boosts their academic achievement), and
- are more likely to finish college.

What makes a great playroom

It doesn't matter how big your play space is or where you put it (ours seems to be the middle of the living room). What matters is that you create opportunities for a variety of experiences.

Think art, science, and imaginative play: Instruments for making music. Clothes for dress-up. Supplies for drawing and creating props. A microscope, a calculator, and kits for science. Newspapers and magazines to cut up. Blocks and more blocks, cardboard boxes and tubes, dolls and cups.

Encourage your child's interests, however random. If your child becomes obsessed with something (garbage trucks, fairies, dinosaurs), riff on the theme.

As often as you can, get into that other wonderful playroom: the great outdoors.

Make-believe

One particular type of play is beneficial to your child's brain. It's play in which children become fully engrossed in pretending to be someone else.

Kids spiritedly discuss who they're going to be and what they're going to do.

"OK, we're going to play house. I'm going to be the mom."

"I want to be the mom!"

"No, I'm the mom and you're the baby, and I'm going to feed you lunch."

"OK, then we take the dog for a walk."

And then they act it out.

It's called mature make-believe play—a serious-sounding name for something so fun. Maybe that's because this type of play is actually quite structured. It requires following the rules of what it means to be a mom or baby, and the steps required to make a meal or walk a dog. If a kid starts wandering outside those rules, the other kids bring him back in line.

What this does for the brain is build executive function: the skill set that allows children to set goals, plan, stay on task, and avoid distraction (see page 116).

In an early-education program called Tools of the Mind, students spend the majority of their time on activities that build executive function— mainly play. In a study of 150 kids, the children in Tools of the Mind classrooms scored 30 percent to nearly 100 percent better on executive-function tests than kids in the control group. They also were

- more creative (asked to think of various uses for specific objects, they came up with three times more ideas),
- more facile with language,
- better at problem solving,
- half as stressed, and
- more socially skilled.

Model how to make-believe

Age 1 to 3: Model pretending

Children are just beginning to learn to play with objects in a pretend way.

Teach your child how to pretend. Take an empty cup and pretend to drink from it. Say, "Let's pretend to make dinner," as you stir a spoon in a pot and then pretend to taste it. Then say, "Now *you* make dinner," and follow what the child does.

Make up a role. "Let's pretend we're ____ (Dad, Grandma, Auntie, Uncle) making dinner." Model what that person would say. "Grandma would say, Do you want cookies for dinner?'" Try to use speech that the child has heard before. Ideally, children will act and sound like the person they are playing.

Set up a play space that is defined, consistent, and accessible. Don't be too quick to put things away.

Have props around, like old clothes and shoes, purses and briefcases, pretend doctors' kits and carpenter tools.

Include blocks and household objects, like cups and spoons, that can become other things with some imagination.

Avoid toys that "do the thinking" for the child. Choose toys that are an easy size for children to manipulate, such as baby dolls that a child can dress and undress, hold, and bathe.

Age 3 to 5: Help with ideas, act out a role

Children have an idea of how to pretend but need ideas of what to pretend.

Use everyday chores, errands, and situations to set up play ideas. Point out people, and talk about what they say and do. Your child can pretend to be them when you get home.

Act out a story your child likes.

Make up props. Don't buy a doctor's uniform—instead, use a grown-up's old shirt and make a stethoscope out of string with a circle attached to it. Creating something symbolic takes more thought.

Follow your child's lead. You want your child to direct the play scene as much as possible, telling you what to do and what will come next. For example, your child could be the doctor and you could be the patient or the father of a sick baby.

Help your child expand the roles and add to the script. "Now, what could happen next? Can we pretend that we had to go to the hospital in an ambulance? What else could happen?"

After playing a role and a scene several times, suggest a new twist. What if you were the doctor on a pirate ship? In outer space? Have the same role happen in a different place.

Introduce simple games with rules. Board games like Chutes and Ladders and Candy Land are an extension of make-believe play.

Age 5 and up: Kids play on their own

Children can act out elaborate scenes by themselves or with other children, using props they created.

You become more of a resource, providing ideas to help get things going, rather than being a part of the play.

Have props available and materials (blocks, pieces of fabric, blankets, paper, scissors, glue) that children can use to make their own props.

Children will begin to play more with little dolls and action figures instead of dressing up and playing the roles themselves. They may engage in "director's play," in which they talk and act for the figures, playing several roles and changing their voices for each of the actors.

Use stories and literature as a basis for play. Encourage children to make their own versions of familiar stories or to make completely new stories, and then act them out.

Play board and card games with simple rules.

If you have more than one child, help the older child teach the younger sibling what to do and say.

Nurture creativity

What will life look like twenty-some years from now, when your baby has grown up?

It's almost impossible to imagine. Our world is so unpredictable that navigating it smartly will require some ingenuity on the part of your children. Creativity will be an important skill for a citizen of this future. Whether your children become entrepreneurs, artists, tradespeople or academics, or work for private enterprises, governments or nonprofits, the world that hires them will be looking for creative thinkers.

Historically, people have used IQ tests to predict a child's success in school and in life beyond. IQ tests give a useful measure of linguistic, logical (mathematical), and spatial abilities. But researchers, entrepreneurs, and educators increasingly agree that creativity—something IQ tests don't measure —is just as valuable in our rapidly changing society.

Can creativity be measured? It can. The Torrance Tests of Creative Thinking have been used for decades by schools to assess students' abilities to create ideas that are original, diverse, and elaborate. One exercise might give a curved line with the instruction "Finish this drawing," for example.

(**DO IT NOW**) When you see a scene during a walk, make a game of guessing what's happening, what caused it, and what might happen next.

Ways to practice creativity

Creative-thinking ability is one-third genetics and two-thirds practice, according to studies of twins separated at birth. Here are ideas for developing creative skills in your child:

- Encourage your child to turn an interest into a passion.
- Allow and encourage mistakes. "If you're not prepared to be wrong, you'll never come up with anything original," notes creativity expert Sir Ken Robinson.
- Sign your child up for visual arts, drama, or reading programs.
- Recognize your child's talents and support them.
- Show more interest in what your children have learned than in their grades.
- Encourage your children to come up with multiple potential solutions for a problem.
- Rather than giving the answers, give your child the tools to find the answers.
- Model the concept of thinking visually: when you have a spatial dilemma, like how to rearrange your furniture, sketch it out with your child.
- Use analogies and metaphors to stimulate new ways of thinking.

Compiled from published interviews with Paul Torrance and Sir Ken Robinson

TRY THIS

How might you help your child turn an interest into a passion? Go all in. If he's drawn to maps, you could plaster his room with maps, play geography games, make a 3-D map of your street out of playdough, hunt for unusual maps at antique shops, use tracing paper to create maps, go geocaching, help him photocopy your city map and chart the route for the day's outings, look at various representations of one location (aerial photos, maps showing topography, climate, or resources), brainstorm how he'd change a map if he were a city planner, take him to visit a cartographer . . .

Ask "Why?" and "What if?"

No one asks more questions than 4-year-olds. And then they go to school.

Children "quickly learn that teachers value the right answers more than provocative questions," says researcher Hal Gregersen in *Harvard Business Review*. "And by the time they're grown up and are in corporate settings, they have already had the curiosity drummed out of them."

How can you create an environment where your child can keep asking "Why?" and "Why not?" and "What if?"

Be a tour guide
Constantly describing and explaining the world around you is one way. I like this story from a stay-at-home dad (who also happens to be a personal-finance blogger):

> I usually spend about six hours a day just playing and learning with my son. I view myself as one of those automated tour guide devices that you can walk around with in a museum—except I'm available to him wherever we are in life.
>
> "Why did the water in the creek flood this dam we made yesterday, Dada?"
>
> "Well, did you notice how it's hot outside today? Look at the thermometer on my watch—86 degrees Fahrenheit, or 30 Celsius. Now look up into the mountains where this creek is coming from. What do you think is happening to the snow on a hot day like today?"

Excerpted with permission from "Avoiding Ivy League Preschool Syndrome," mrmoneymustache.com

I try to do the same with my toddler. She loves talking about bicycles, putting on helmets, and spinning the pedals of bikes we pass on the sidewalk. So when my bike tire got a flat, I let her squeeze each tire to feel the difference, help me pull off the tire, and push the air pump. It was more interesting for both of us than shooing her away from the dirty job.

Another day, when she kept getting into some tea candles on a closet shelf, I took one into a dark room. She sat in my lap as I lit it. We talked quietly about how beautiful fire is, and how a flame is hot if you touch it. She held a tiny finger over the flame before pulling away: a baby's version of playing with fire.

Why not?

WHY? WHY? WHY? WHY? WHY?

If you're feeling trapped in an endless series of questions, consider that your preschooler isn't always asking you for an answer. Sometimes it's a way of telling you that he noticed something, says play therapist Garry Landreth. Try responding, "You noticed that" or "You're wondering about that." See where the conversation goes.

Connect

Mini manifesto: Let's spend more time on the floor with our kids. Let's trade strollers for newborn carriers, and car trips for walks. Let's spend more time looking into each other's eyes, and less time staring into our screens. Let's really get to know each other.

Ask for help

"I feel like I should be able to handle it."

That's what my neighbor said in explaining why she hadn't taken me up on my offer to babysit. "No, it's OK," another friend said as she juggled both kids into the restaurant bathroom instead of leaving me to entertain one kid in her high chair.

It's hard to ask for help. We don't want to burden anyone, or we think needing help is a failure on our part, that we're supposed to be able to handle this parenting thing by ourselves.

If something is keeping you from asking for help, please get over it.

Imagine if a friend asked *you* for help. You would be more than happy to oblige (unless your baby is 0 to 6 months old, in which case you're still in shock).

But we have collectively forgotten that it is impossible to raise another human without help. It's not an issue of whether you're mentally tough enough to do it. Our species did not evolve to raise children solo, and only relatively recently has it become a typical experience. Over and over, I've seen unrealistic self-expectations lead to isolation, depression, desperation, or guilt.

Many hands make light work

I didn't truly understand what "It takes a village to raise a child" means until I found myself in a two-bedroom hotel suite on a weekend away with my toddler, mom, two sisters, 14-year-old niece, and 9-year-old nephew. As we reconnected over hair talk, impromptu makeovers, and family stories, my baby ran around the suite. Whoever was nearby watched her. What a difference! The burden wasn't too great on any one of us. It felt fantastic. And I felt that sense of relief even though I have an incredibly helpful husband, ten hours a week of babysitting, dear friends, and a lot of patience.

If you haven't spent much time around babies before you had your own (I hadn't), your idea of how much work a baby takes may be waaaay off. In one tribal culture, it's not uncommon for *fourteen* people to watch a baby in an eight-hour span. So build more of a support network than you think you need.

Unless your parents or siblings are planning to move in next door, you'll need to build a community through friends and neighbors. (See page 8 for ideas.) Once you've done that, actually use it.

My neighbor and I agreed that she would have accepted my offer to babysit if I had more aggressively inserted myself, as in: "I'm free to borrow your baby on Thursday. What time is good for you?" So that's what I said the next time I offered—and she said, "Noon."

(**DO IT NOW**) Ask!

Choose empathy first

Here's one of the best things you can do for your marriage: in an emotional situation, make empathy your first response.

We often jump to offer advice, play devil's advocate, defend the person upsetting our partner, or change the subject. All our partner really wants is empathy: for us to identify with what they're feeling. So truly listen. Show that you understand how your partner feels.

"I'm sorry. I hate it when that happens. I can understand how that would be frustrating."

"Oh, baby, that is so disappointing. I know you had your heart set on that."

"I hear you. That never feels good."

What empathy does
Empathy literally calms the body. The brain uses the vagus nerve to monitor and control the state of your organs. When your brain senses empathy, it signals the vagus nerve to relax your body by slowing your heart rate or lowering your blood pressure.

Why empathy is key to relationships

Empathy is powerful in a marriage because a resolution doesn't exist for the majority of disagreements. The people involved simply have differing values, motivations, or desires. Your best path through the conflict is to simply show understanding.

One of the perpetual conflicts my husband and I have is that I'm a night owl and he's an early riser. If I stayed up too late, my husband used to lecture me about personal responsibility. But he's more empathetic these days.

"Did you sleep OK?" he asked.

"No, maybe four hours," I said. "I stayed up too late."

"I'm sorry," he said. "What can I do to help?"

The first time I got that kind of response, relief and gratitude flowed through me. I felt supported instead of attacked. I felt closer to my husband instead of at odds with him. That's kind of amazing for eight little words.

TRY THIS

Choosing empathy first with our newborn, too, was a big help. Considering baby's perspective (as often as we could) kept us from growing irritated over spending yet another hour bouncing baby, or changing yet another diaper in the middle of the night. My husband was good at this. "I'm sorry you're sad," he would tell our crying newborn. "It must be hard to be a baby." Or "Let's change your diaper. I know I always feel better with a clean diaper." That always made me laugh.

Empathy works well as baby gets older, too. If your child wants something he can't have, for example,
try saying, "Yes, you want that. It's so hard to want something you can't have."

Or "Yes, you want more blueberries. They taste so good, you never want to stop! And uh-oh, it's time to stop now. Later will work."

Or "That's a screwdriver. It's a tool that we only use together. I will show you."

Baby feels heard, and your conversation is saved from being a frustrating series of "No, don't touch that," "No, don't do that," and "No, you can't have that."

Create more ups than downs

....

Every marriage has conflicts.

It doesn't matter whether the two of you tend to calmly compromise, have big blow-ups and then make up, or rarely confront your differences. All three styles of dealing with inevitable conflicts can make for happy, stable relationships.

The important thing, marriage researcher John Gottman says, is that your marriage has more positive interactions (touching, smiling, complimenting, etc.) than negative ones. In happy marriages, it's a five-to-one ratio. Not that you're keeping track, exactly.

Summarizing thirty-five years of research, Gottman says happily married couples

- behave like good friends,
- handle their conflicts in gentle and positive ways,
- repair negative interactions during an argument, and
- fully process negative emotions.

On the flip side, Gottman found four corrosive behaviors that, if couples engage in them regularly, lead to divorce in an average of five and a half years:

Criticism: stating your complaints as a personality defect in your partner. For example: "You always leave messes lying around for me to clean up. Why do you have to be so lazy?" rather than, "I would appreciate it if we could do the dishes together."

Contempt: making statements from a position of superiority, often while thinking that the other person is a total moron ("*That's* not the right way to do it").

Defensiveness: denying responsibility ("I wouldn't have . . . if you hadn't . . ."), blaming circumstances beyond your control, or immediately responding with a complaint of your own ("You're not perfect, either"), rather than acknowledging your partner's complaint.

Stonewalling: instead of giving the usual signals that you're listening (nodding, "mm-hmm," "go on"), you sit in stony silence.

> *"Rather than becoming defensive and hurtful, [masters of marriage] pepper their disputes with flashes of affection, intense interest, and mutual respect."*
>
> **John Gottman, The Relationship Cure**

It's how you handle your conflicts—not a lack of conflict—that makes for a good relationship. The same thing is true of your relationship with your kids.

THE RESEARCH

John Gottman, one of the nation's leading marriage and parenting researchers, runs the "Love Lab" at the University of Washington. He has predicted with 94 percent success whether couples will stay together. Gottman has studied more than three thousand couples in researching why some marriages end in divorce and others remain strong.

Know your child

Children all have their own temperaments.

Some babies are calm, cool, and collected. They'll eat everything from beet borscht to coconut quinoa. Raining? Sunny? Great. They want to be outside. If they get upset, it doesn't last. If you explain how something works, they generally accept it. If you show them something, they want to try it.

Other babies are much more sensitive to change. They like to eat the same thing at the same time in the same way. They hang back. They startle and cry at an unfamiliar toy or person. On the flip side, they are fiercely loyal, given time. They're cautious about trying to do new things.

Still other babies run headfirst into whatever interests them—and everything interests them. They have boundless energy; their parents become sprinters, on-the-alert anticipators, and rapid redirectors. They're incredibly persistent. Sensitive to change, their moods are intense.

They were just born this way.

Researchers Stella Chess and Alexander Thomas were the first to categorize temperament. Collecting data on nearly 140 children from 1956 to 1988, Thomas and Chess identified nine dimensions of temperament: activity, regularity, initial reaction, adaptability, intensity, mood, distractibility, persistence/attention span, and sensitivity.

Because of this work, researchers now recognize that babies are born with a temperament, that it is fairly stable throughout childhood, that parents have only limited influence over it, and that it influences one's parenting style, too.

Thomas and Chess found that 65 percent of children fell into the following three categories, and the rest of the children were a combination:

TYPES OF TEMPERMENT

Flexible / Easy-going 40% of children	Feisty / Spirited 10% of children	Cautious / Slow to warm up 15% of children
pretty adaptable	don't adapt easily to change	don't adapt easily to change
regular patterns of eating and sleeping	irregular patterns of eating and sleeping	regular or irregular patterns of eating and sleeping
approach new stimuli with ease	withdraw from new stimuli	withdraw from new stimuli
react mildly to change	react intensely to change	initially react mildly to change, but form an opinion after multiple exposures

No one temperament is better than another

Of the nine dimensions Thomas and Chess identified, no one aspect is ideal in all situations. Persistence might help your child make the team, and at the same time wear you down during disagreements. Shyness might protect your child from becoming a troublemaker, and at the same time mean your child misses out on opportunities in school.

While temperament may remain relatively stable, baby's expression of it doesn't. A shy child can learn to become more comfortable socially with gentle guidance, for example. Researcher Jerome Kagan found that children at the extreme ends of the spectrum migrate toward the middle by age 7.

Temperament doesn't predict who your child will become so much as it predicts who your child will not become.

Creating a good fit
What will you think of your baby's temperament? That depends on your own. Any temperament will seem difficult to deal with if it doesn't fit your own values, style, and expectations.

"Goodness of fit," Thomas and Chess called it.

If you and baby aren't naturally a good fit, you can create a better one by adjusting your expectations, your style, and baby's environment (such as finding ways for a rambunctious child to spend more time outdoors). Even if you and baby are a good fit, it takes time to get to know your child and understand how to parent accordingly.

For example, my toddler seemed confident trying new things, so I assumed she would feel immediately comfortable joining a group of new people. I'd plop her in the middle and step to the side. She would come hug my leg. I would be a little disappointed. Soon I figured out that I needed to sit with her or hold her for a minute, and then she'd happily join in.

Temperamental baby
No matter baby's temperament, baby is sometimes going to be temperamental. There's the evening "witching hour," when for some reason newborns get super fussy and nothing you do helps.

There's the sudden appearance of toddlers' insistent "*No!*" to whatever you do ("No, that's *my* leg!" as I put on baby's pants). And as baby's sense of self continues to emerge, there's the stubborn "By self!" or "*I* do it!"—especially when you don't have time for baby to "do it."

Parenting a feisty baby

"Feisty" kids are the most challenging for anyone to parent, as they tend to be irritable and react grandly to small things. Some things you can do to help:

Stay engaged. Over time, studies show, mothers tend to withdraw from highly reactive babies, increasingly ignoring them and playing less with them. Counteract this tendency by approaching each encounter with empathy and an understanding that the most important thing is for baby to feel safe.

Get coaching. In one study, parents of "feisty" 6-month-olds received three months of training in being sensitive to their child's needs. At 12 months old, 70 percent of those infants were deemed securely attached, compared with 30 percent of infants whose parents didn't receive training. You can seek out for a parenting class or a parent coach for support. Good books include *Say What You See for Parents and Teachers* by Sandy Blackard and *Raising Your Spirited Child* by Mary Sheedy Kurcinka.

Commit to consistency. Parents of highly reactive children tend to become inconsistent in their discipline, which leads to a more highly reactive child.

Defuse conflicts. If both child and mother have highly reactive temperaments, the child is likely to become more, not less, defiant and aggressive. When you get upset, call a time-out (or calm-down) for yourself (see page 199) to avoid escalating conflicts.

TRY THIS

Many of my friends get anxious that I let my baby tackle a climbing wall for bigger kids or let her roam a little farther outdoors. And I get anxious that they don't let their babies do these things. Of course, each of us knows our babies, and we're usually doing the right things for them (and us).

But as new parents, uncertain of our choices, it's easy to feel judged.

Try heading off the disapproval of others by helping them understand your baby. "She likes to watch first. She knows when she is ready, so it's best if you hang back and let her come to you," you might say of a shy baby. Or "Yes, he's a feisty one. We really admire that he puts his whole heart into things."

Hold weekly family meetings

When are you going to talk about how things are working (or not working) in your family?

While you're all rushing off to school and work? In the middle of a tantrum or argument? During the one meal you eat together, when you'd rather talk about everyone's day?

Try a twenty-minute weekly family meeting instead. According to Bruce Feiler in *The Secrets of Happy Families*, devotees report

- less stress, more communication, and more productivity;
- kids coming up with creative solutions to their own problems; and
- calmer decision making ("I see you're upset about this. Let's put it on our family-meeting agenda").

How it works

Set a day and time, like Sunday evenings, that you promise not to schedule over. The meeting should focus on the family as a unit rather than on individuals. Involve the kids around age 3.

Ask three questions:

1. **What worked well in our family this past week?**
   You could start by having each family member compliment every other family member: "I liked it when . . ." or "I appreciated that . . ."
2. **What went wrong in our family this past week?**
   Keep it civil.

3. **What will we work on this coming week?**

   Choose one or two problems to focus on, and brainstorm solutions together. Don't shoot down any of the ideas right away; that shuts down creative thinking. Get all of the ideas out there, evaluate them as a family, and choose one solution together. Agree to try it out for a certain amount of time, then reevaluate it at a later family meeting.

Allow a few weeks for everyone to practice and get comfortable with the concept. Afterward, some families watch a movie or go for ice cream, so the idea of a weekly meeting is more fun.

PROBLEM SOLVED

Wasted food on the plate after dinner: that was the agenda item at the Natkin family's weekly meeting. During their brainstorming session, the children came up with several ideas:

"Why don't we count the food?" (Mom was thinking: Individual peas, or what?)

"Why don't we serve dinner family-style?" (Mom was thinking: Uh, we already do that.)

"Let's weigh the food!"

OK, everyone agreed, worth a shot. So each night after the plates were dished up, and then again after dinner, each plate was weighed. They tracked and posted each person's numbers.

"I didn't think the idea was going to work," Sarina Natkin says. "But better to try it out."

Within three nights, food waste plummeted. The kids were either serving themselves less food or eating more; either way, the tracking had created awareness and accountability. Soon they didn't have to weigh the plates anymore. Natkin was amazed.

"Going through this process together as a family," she says, "does so much more to shift behavior than me saying, 'This is what's going to happen.'"

Put down your phone

I can hear your sputters of protest already:
Is such an *extreme* measure *really* necessary?

Science can't tell you for sure. There is no definitive research (yet) about the effects of smartphones and other digital devices. But we do know a few important things about ourselves as humans, and these things can help inform how and when you use your phone.

We are social animals. We thrive on face-to-face interaction, and we don't function well without it. Human interaction is so important that, in baby's first years, it is what turns on the brain for certain types of learning (see page 71).

The most important thing in your child's life is his or her relationships. With you, with siblings, with friends; eventually with classmates and teachers, with colleagues and bosses, with romantic partners, with his or her own children. What makes for good relationships? Things you learn through lots of face-to-face interaction: communication skills, empathy, and control over your emotions and behavior. A large part of communication is nonverbal: interpreting facial expressions, gestures, and body language.

Children need a ton of practice reading other people. Studies show how much time it takes to understand nonverbal communication:

- Three-year-olds are better than 2-year-olds at understanding the facial expressions that add meaning to an utterance (such as a look implying "you need to do this" with a directive to clean up the toys).
- Four-year-olds are able to identify and communicate emotions in body movement at a rate better than chance; 5-year-olds are even better at it.
- Eight-year-olds are as good at reading nonverbal signs as adults.

Children can't practice reading people if one (or both) of you is buried in a device.

Great relationships are the secret to happiness. Being truly present with your child, partner, and friends makes for more fulfilling relationships. And that's the key to the good life.

PHONE BAN

I have a personal ban on checking my phone or opening up my laptop when baby's around.

I fail at least once a day. But I can see that it's worth trying. I can tell that my digital devices suck me in for longer than I intend. And I can tell that my baby is upset about being ignored—just as I am when I'd like to communicate with someone and they're more entranced by a glowing screen.

So I'll send a quick text message in the kitchen while baby's busy in her high chair. I may check in just before a run, when she's facing away in the jogging stroller. I've turned off the automatic e-mail sync, so I don't see a visual indicator on my phone that I have e-mail, and feel the need to read it right then. My phone is often set to vibrate, so it's not a distraction. My laptop is tucked away until nap time or bedtime.

I'm not saying we should avoid digital devices entirely. But it is worth considering how much of our time they should take up, and how and when they should be used (see page 154).

These days, it takes effort to create conditions that encourage, not discourage, real live interaction.

(Almost) no TV before age 2

What's so wrong with a little TV? Most people would say, "Nothing."

That must be why 40 percent of babies are watching TV by 3 months old, and 90 percent of tots are watching one to two hours of TV or videos per day by age 2.

When the American Academy of Pediatrics issued its 1996 policy statement on TV for kids, most media reported AAP's stance as "zero TV before age 2." That's widely seen as unrealistic. In a 2013 update, the AAP "discourages" TV.

Either way, what's the problem with TV for baby? A few things.

- **There are no known positive effects of babies watching TV.** Not even educational videos marketed for infants. The human brain is wired to learn from humans, at least early on. Face-to-face interaction literally acts like a gatekeeper for the brain, determining whether certain kinds of learning will happen—or not.
- **TV hurts language skills.** Babies who watched *Baby Einstein* videos knew fewer vocabulary words than babies who didn't watch. The study results were such a reversal of the product's claims that Disney, who produced the videos, offered refunds to parents. Two studies found that *Sesame Street* hurt expressive language for kids under age 2 (although after age 2 it helped in other areas, such as school readiness).
- **When the TV is on, babies aren't interacting.** Kids don't get face-to-face interaction. They're not hearing you talk. They're not exploring or playing or moving—key activities for development.

Baby isn't interacting . . . um, that's the point, right? TV isn't *for* the baby; it's for the break *from* baby. It gets a toddler to sit still for thirty minutes instead of, for example, emptying all the drawers while you're trying to clean the house. "Educational" videos just make you feel less guilty about it.

Perhaps the real issues are these:

Parents need a break, and we're not asking for the help we need from our partners, neighbors, family, and friends. (see pages 8 and page 134 for ideas.)

Parents want to get stuff done. This is so much easier when baby is otherwise occupied. But it's less stressful if we can align our expectations with our new reality. Knowing baby is the priority when you're together avoids the tension created by competing priorities. Sure, we'll get less done. Yes, any task will take five times longer. On the other hand, what's truly wrong with that?

A TINY BIT OF TV

My husband and I have a no-TV policy. Sure, our baby has seen some TV. There was the time a sitter asked if the baby could watch videos on her cell phone, then let it slip: "She loves it!" We've visited folks accustomed to having the TV on during dinner, and we've made exceptions for sports play-off games.

But I like our TV ban. It definitely makes us more aware of when a TV is on. And it's clear that baby gets more (and more interesting) interaction from us when the TV is off. That fits with research showing that when the TV is on, parents' interaction with their kids drops by 20 percent.

I'm also relieved that the AAP's policy isn't a complete ban. One less thing to feel guilty about.

A little TV after age 2

After age 2, kids can learn something valuable from interactive TV shows.

Look for shows where the characters

- speak directly to your child,
- provide opportunities for your child to respond, and
- label objects.

Educational shows with those characteristics, like *Blue's Clues* and *Dora the Explorer*, can improve vocabulary, social skills, and school readiness. Common Sense Media (commonsensemedia.org) has ratings and reviews to help you choose.

What's so magical about age 2? Somewhere between 18 months and 30 months, researchers found, a child's ability to process information changes, and kids are better able to focus attention on TV. With repeated exposure to a screen, kids learn how to extract information from it.

Vocabulary
Interactive shows, like *Dora the Explorer* and *Blue's Clues*, were able to teach kids vocabulary words, one study found. Non-interactive shows, like *Barney & Friends* or Disney movies, weren't.

Social skills

Pop quiz: Should your 3-year-old watch the crude adult cartoon *King of the Hill*? Or Nickelodeon's *Wonder Pets!* show about team players? One study shows that you can reduce physical aggression in preschoolers by switching aggressively themed adult shows to children's shows with a pro-social message (showing empathy, helping others, or resolving disputes without violence).

School readiness

Low-income and moderate-income kids who watched educational shows (like *Sesame Street, Mister Rogers,* and *3-2-1 Contact*) had higher academic test scores three years later than kids who didn't watch the shows.

DIGITAL DEVICES: TWO EMERGING GUIDELINES

The more social a technology is, the better. If two children touch a screen together, for example, they learn twice as much as they do when they're flying solo.

The more responsive a technology is, the more a child can learn from it. If children have to touch the screen in order to hear snippets of language, for example, they learn more than from a passive experience.

The trouble with two-plus hours a day of TV

Children can learn from a screen, but the American Academy of Pediatrics still recommends less than two hours a day of time in front of a TV—or any other screen—for children older than 2. Here's why:

Time spent watching TV predicts obesity. When kids are watching TV, they're eating more and exercising less. Watching TV is so passive that one's metabolic rate drops even lower than when sitting at a desk. More than two hours of TV or videos a day is a health risk.

Kids miss out on reading. In families where the TV is almost always on (and that's 30 percent of families with young kids), reading time gets shafted by 25 percent at ages 3 and 4, and nearly 40 percent at ages 5 and 6, compared to other families.

Background TV distracts kids from play. When the TV is on in the background, kids may not appear to be paying attention to it, glancing at the TV only sporadically. But between ages 1 and 3, the kids play for less time, are less focused during play, skip from one toy to another, and play in a less sophisticated way. (See page 116 for the importance of play.)

Attention spans shorten. Kids who watch more than two hours of TV per day, studies show, appear to have more trouble focusing attention.

TV disrupts sleep. Kids who watch more than two hours a day of TV are much more likely to have sleep problems. TV at night is no good, either. Nearly 30 percent of children ages 2 to 3 have a TV in their room, and those parents say it helps their kid sleep. But studies show that it actually puts off bedtime, puts off falling asleep, makes kids more anxious about sleep, and shortens the time spent sleeping. Lack of sleep is bad for baby's long-term learning ability, not to mention mood and behavior the next day.

Other potential pitfalls

Preschoolers are particularly harmed by violent shows. That's likely because social norms haven't set in, kids at this age imitate so readily, and their social development is more malleable.

Kids are indiscriminate imitators. After watching one game of football, our 19-month-old (with more than a little encouragement from her dad) would raise both arms sky-high and squeal, "Touchy-down!" Cute. Less cute is that she would dive-bomb the floor and try to smack my head with hers. Between ages 2 and 5, kids are still working on differentiating fantasy from reality. They'll imitate "even the most unrealistic behavior patterns," as one study puts it. So are your kids watching things you want them to mimic?

Kids may not get the message. In one study, kids who watched educational TV became, over time, increasingly aggressive—not physically, but in their inter-personal relationships. (Like withholding a birthday-party invitation if the other child doesn't fulfill a request, or excluding a child from the group.)

These TV shows set up a conflict, usually based on interpersonal aggression, with a reconciliation at the end. But the kids, left to watch on their own, focused on the conflict and missed the moral of the story.

An episode of the show *Clifford the Big Red Dog*, for example, was intended to teach that friendship overcomes physical differences (one dog had three legs). But 90 percent of kindergarteners in a study couldn't identify the intended message.

TRY THIS

Make a list, together with your kids, of things they can do besides watch TV. Read and discuss The Berenstain Bears and Too Much TV. *Turn off the TV for a week. Help children make "No TV" signs for each TV set. Do the fun things on your list.*

Make screen time social

Watch with your kids.

The best way to mitigate the negatives and boost the positives of screen time?
Make it a social interaction.

- During a show, ask open-ended questions. "Why do you think he feels sad?"
- Connect what you see to real life. "I remember when we went to the zoo. You especially liked the elephant."
- When the show is over, recap. "So Dora had to get to school. She tried so many ways to get there! Do you remember all of them?" "What was your favorite part?" "What was that about?"
- If video games are your thing, play together. Acknowledge the thrill of victory, the agony of defeat, and the persistence it takes to win.

Other ways to be thoughtful about screens

Set time limits. Play, exercise, face-to-face interaction, the outdoors, sleep—these are so important for your child's healthy development. Once you fit them into the day, how much time is left for screens? Pediatricians officially recommend less than two hours a day. In their own families, though, many experts limit screen time to two hours a week—often on weekends only. The important thing is intentionally setting a limit, one that works for your family.

Choose the content. Decide which shows, websites, apps, and games your child will be allowed to access. Watch them yourself first. Common Sense Media (commonsensemedia.org) also has ratings and reviews.

Hold off. There's no evidence that not using devices will put your tot at an educational disadvantage. Older kids figure out the intuitive interfaces just as quickly.

If you see signs of dependence on a device, put it away. Parenting coach Sandy Blackard says the device has become better than real life at meeting your child's need for connection and power. Increase time with friends, she recommends, and opportunities for your child to set his own level of challenge (see pages page 45 and page 160).

Consider your habits. How much screen time will your kids consume as they grow older? The single most defining factor—more than the rules you set, or whether you watch as a family, or whether your kids have a TV in their room— is how much screen time *you* consume. (Most families are fine with that amount.)

Enhance, don't replace, real-world learning. One family who was raising caterpillars looked up time-lapse videos of a butterfly metamorphosis. Pretty cool.

Encourage mistakes, discomfort, and boredom

It's hard to see your baby unhappy. But if you solve every problem for her, she can't learn how to solve problems herself.

A friend and I were ready to leave when our toddlers decided they wanted to zip up each other's jackets. You can imagine our agony. My friend and I practically had to bite our fingernails to keep from just zipping the darn things ourselves. But we managed. The girls got it. And they were so, so proud. We parents want to send our children the message that they are capable. But what message do we actually send when we hover and too-quickly interfere?

Here are some strategies for developing baby's self-sufficiency:

Wait. When your toddler is trying to unscrew a lid, do you give him three seconds and then jump in? Take a minute, pull him onto your lap, and just wait. You might say, "Yep, twist left to open. Oops, if you twist left and right, the lid doesn't come off, huh?" If he gets close, say enthusiastically, "Almost!" You'll know when he's ready to give up. Ask, "Would you like help?" Then you might put your fingers over his and let him feel the motion of unscrewing the lid.

Show, don't just tell. When your 3-year-old declines to put on his coat, stand outside with him for a minute. "Why don't we check the weather. Brr! It's cold outside, isn't it! Let's put on our coats so we can be nice and warm."

Accept uncomfortable emotions. Label the feelings embarrassment, shame, guilt, and humility—not just the easy feelings. When *you* feel those things, say so. Allow your child to feel them, rather than being dismissive. Empathize. Don't jump to protect your child from tough feelings. Talk about how emotions feel in the body. Show how acknowledging intense feelings—with our words ("I'm feeling angry") and our bodies (sobbing, breathing, dancing)—helps them pass.

Free up some free time. If you pack your children's day with activities and access to glowing screens, they don't have enough space to get bored—and then learn for themselves how to while away the time. When always-busy kids don't feel occupied, they grow agitated. They look to you to fill their time, because they haven't learned how to fill it themselves.

Boredom is a frustrating and restless state; the brain wants to get out of it. So, given practice, the brain will find constructive things to do: daydream, imagine, think through a problem, plan. That's why researchers say boredom can be central to learning and creativity. So next time you hear "I'm booored!" try some variation of, "Mmm. I'm reading right now. What's *your* plan?"

Guide

Our job is to guide our children toward lifelong skills: good communication, empathy, emotional awareness, and respect for others. When we point out the good in our kids, we get more of it. The best approach to discipline is both firm and kind—not "Do what I say, or else."

Be firm but warm

A certain style of parenting tends to produce kids who are

- more self-reliant,
- more self-confident,
- more socially competent,
- less anxious, and
- less depressed.

These parents are attuned to and supportive of their children's needs, and they firmly but respectfully enforce their rules. Researcher Diana Baumrind of UC-Berkeley refers to this parenting style as "authoritative."

Study after study since the mid-1980s shows strong correlations between parenting style and a child's positive—or not-so-positive—social behavior.

That's not to say parenting style *guarantees* a certain type of child. Our influence on the way our kids turn out is limited. We're competing, of course, with genetics, peers, culture, and the other adults (nannies, teachers, grandparents, coaches) in our children's lives. Parents can claim maybe 20 percent to 50 percent of the influence, researchers say.

But we do what we can, right?

A CONTINUUM OF PARENTING STYLES

Authoritarian parents are firm but not warm. They have strict rules and expect their orders to be obeyed without empathy: "Why? Because I said so." Their children tend to be well behaved, but they are less able to develop critical self-regulation skills (see page 116). They also fall short in moral-reasoning abilities, because their sense of right and wrong is guided by external forces—threat of punishment—rather than internal principles.

Authoritative parents are both firm and warm, with high expectations. They model respect. They intentionally foster individuality and self-assertion. For example, when they set rules, they invite discussion about the parameters of those rules. When the rules are broken, they find out why and work to solve problems collaboratively. They aim to guide instead of punish. Their goal is a young adult who has self-control, emotional awareness, problem-solving skills, and strong internal principles.

Permissive parents are warm but not firm. They are nurturing and communicative, but also indulgent. They avoid confrontation and are reluctant to enforce their rules. Their children often have an inflated sense of self. The children tend to be more impulsive, more likely to abuse drugs and alcohol, and more likely to get into trouble at school.

Uninvolved parents are neither firm nor warm. They provide for their children's basic needs but are otherwise disengaged. Their children are the most likely to be delinquent.

What's your parenting style?

Your parenting style will be influenced by your child's temperament, by your own temperament, by how *you* were parented, and by what other parents around you are doing. (And by whether your child just popped out of her room at bedtime for the third time or for the thirteenth time.) So think of it as a spectrum, not an absolute.

It's easier to be authoritarian, to yell or threaten or spank and be done with it. Being authoritative takes more time, effort, and patience. So give yourself room to mess up and try again next time, especially if you're not a patient person or you don't have authoritative parents as role models.

Choosing a certain parenting style, rather than reacting impulsively, may really take work. I find myself making small corrections every day. In the end, it's up to you and your partner to keep your values in mind (see page 30), and make the choice. You can also get support from a counselor, parent coach, or parent-education class.

Why we might choose one style but revert to another

Wonder why it's hard to act the way we intend to act in the moment? Here's the short list:

The situation may be triggering something from our own childhood, and we lash out even as we think, "What am I doing?"

Maybe our minds start spiraling: *My child is disrespecting me, getting out of bed again when I told him to stay there. What, my kid can't stay quiet for 20 minutes? He's going to be the disruptive one in the classroom someday. Now he won't get the rest he needs. I need him to have this quiet time! When is he going to appreciate everything I'm doing for him?* And those thoughts are the things we're really reacting to.

Maybe we feel the hot gaze of another parent and, in our need to prove we're *handling this*, we overreact or do what we think the other parent expects.

Likely our emotional reserves are incredibly depleted, especially by the time our kids are 2 or 3. We're probably not getting as many breaks as we need or taking great care of ourselves. Even tougher, our children's imitation of us can be a mirror we'd rather not see, forcing us to rethink who we are and change. And change again. And again. Enlightening but exhausting.

On top of it all, kids decline to do what we want in the most minor situations. So many times a day. Especially when we're running late.

These are the things that flip our lids (see page 170). When we flip to our animal brains, we go straight to our default reaction: how we were raised. That's not always how we hope to parent.

It's so challenging. Yet getting this right feels serious, doesn't it? We know our reaction directly affects the way our children will react to the tough situations in their own lives. Our reaction directly affects our relationship with our children, now and as adults. It creates the day-to-day feel of our households: safe and loving, or harsh and stressful. Fortunately, it's what we do MOST of the time that matters.

In the moment, the first step is simply: Stop. Name the emotion out loud: "I'm feeling so frustrated." Breathe. Then respond. If it's too late for that, it's never too late to apologize, to repair, and try again next time.

WHAT PARENTING STYLES SOUND LIKE

Authoritarian	Authoritative
"Hey! Don't cut in line. Move out of the way; let that kid go first."	"You want a turn. Yours is right after theirs. You can wait in line here."
"We're leaving now." If kid keeps playing, picks him up and goes.	"In five minutes, it will be time to go." "What's the one thing you want to do before we go? Slide? That's OK with me." If kid keeps playing, picks him up and goes.
"Stop and put your shoe back on."	"Good problem solving! Your shoe came off, but you figured out how to keep climbing."
"Get over here. Apologize right now. Do that again and you'll be sorry."	"You were angry and hit him. Now he's crying. That's not what you wanted. Hmm. Must be some way to play together without hitting. You can try apologizing and starting over."
"Sit down."	"You want to stand, and strollers are for sitting. You can stand and push with me, or sit and ride."
"You're still hungry? Sorry, you already had a snack. The rule is one."	"You're still hungry? OK, you can eat these cucumbers or one piece of cheese."

Permissive

Watches child cut in line. Apologizes to other parent with a little laugh.

"It's time to go now, OK?" If kid keeps playing, parent sits there.

"I think you should put your shoe back on?"

"If you hit someone again, we're going to leave. What did I tell you? Don't do that again. Do you want to leave? I asked you not to hit people. I said stop. Do you want to leave? Hit again and we'll leave."

"Please sit down. It would be better if you sat down. OK, you can stand for just a little bit."

"You're still hungry? OK, eat what you want."

Follow four rules about rules

Kids need boundaries to feel safe and to provide a guide to the world.

1. Make your rules clear and consistent

We must be consistent for boundaries to be effective over the long term. And we are talking long term. It takes *forever* for the brain to turn knowledge into automatic action. So our goal, perhaps surprisingly, is not immediate obedience. That goal would conflict with the way the brain develops, setting everyone up for failure. Our goal is to provide boundaries, and then help our children succeed at following them.

Sometimes being consistent is easy. Helping my preschooler wear clothes outside is something I do every time. Sometimes I'm not so quick. For example, as a toddler, my daughter liked to stand on the dining table. Oh, she knew the rule. Even as she hoisted a leg up, she'd shake her head and say, "No climbing onna table." If I stopped her every single time, that would be much more effective than if I *almost* always stopped her but occasionally laughed at the little tap dance she did up there. (Can you tell I totally messed that up?)

If we're inconsistent, our children will be confused about whether it's really a boundary.

To make rules clear: Keep them short and sweet. Say what you want to happen—not what you don't want to happen. Compare "No climbing on the table" to "At the table, we sit." Which one makes it easier to know what to do?

Even when you are consistent, your child will test a rule again and again to learn its relative importance, to establish the limits of his independence, to see your reaction—and maybe to try to get that laugh out of you one more time.

2. Give the reason for the rule

Your child will be far more likely to internalize a rule if you add just one line: the explanation for it.

"We always close the screen door."

"We always close the screen door. It keeps the cat from running away."

The second rule sounds a lot more reasonable, right? (Except when you harp on it in the middle of misbehavior. This is for calm times or demonstrating something yourself.)

Children who hear reasons for rules are able to make the connection between the rule and the behavior: "I should (or shouldn't) do that because [whatever reason you gave]." Over time, this thought process allows your child to incorporate the rule into her own set of values, consider other applications for the rule, and eventually comply with the rule even when no one is looking.

Children who don't hear reasons for rules, and are punished for breaking them, can draw only one conclusion:

"I shouldn't (or should) do that because I'll get in trouble." Their behavior ends up being guided by an external threat of punishment rather than by an internal set of morals. Strong morals—the personal beliefs we use to judge right and wrong—provide kids with an important set of tools for navigating the world as they grow up.

3. Help your children succeed

Like us—except far more often—kids forget things, get distracted, and make mistakes. They need our help.

Practice together. Take the time to show your child what success looks like to you. Parent coach Sandy Blackard calls this "success training." Her example:

"You still want to bang your toy right on the floor. A cushion underneath doesn't work for you, and the floor's not OK with me." Show the boundary is real by catching the toy. Help her succeed in stopping herself: "You're pulling it; trying to bang it again. Show me stopping yourself." Hold on until you feel less resistance, and point that out. "There. You stopped a little. I felt it. Show me more stopping. There! That was even more! Tell me when you are ready for ALL stopping. Now? OK."

If she succeeds, name a strength: "There! You did it!" If not, offer a can-do: "Uh-oh! Still trying to bang. Hmm. I can put it away and you can try later, or you can try ALL stopping one more time now." If she succeeds, name a strength. If not, remove the toy and say, "You can try again after lunch." If she gets upset, help her let her feelings out. You can hold her while she cries. Or say what you see with empathy: "You really wanted to bang the toy." "You're stomping! You know how to get your anger out."

Prompt your children just before a situation they've been struggling with; say your child hits during playdates or begs while shopping.

"What's our rule about asking over and over for toys at the store? Will that be easy or hard for you today?" "If you begin to feel mad at your friend, what can you do?" This helps children engage critical thought and invites them to practice self-regulation.

If they struggle: Say what you see (see page 176).

Notice behavior you want. You will get more of it. "You're playing with gentle hands." "You know how to take turns." "You're helping me shop only for things on our list. I know it's hard. You're really showing self-control."

Note the lack of judgment here: you're just saying what you see, then naming a strength (see page 176).

4. Set rules together

Have you ever had a boss who commanded your every move and didn't want to hear your input? It feels horrible. You practically want to rebel out of spite. It also sets up a power struggle: neither person wants to lose, and whoever does is bound to resent it.

Don't be that boss. Instead, involve your children in setting rules (making sure agreements don't feel coerced). It's important to do this when everyone is calm, not in the middle of some rule breaking. The process makes your children feel respected, valued, and treated fairly. Plus, their good ideas might surprise you. Go team!

Set a time to talk. Say your child is spending more time than you'd like in front of the TV. You tell him so, and that at dinner you'll talk about creating some rules around screen time.

Frame the problem. Together with your child, list the priorities for the afternoon: homework, dinner, playing, reading, bedtime. "Looks to me," you say, "like we have twenty minutes per day for TV." Get input: "What else would you like me to consider?"

Encourage input on aspects where you can be flexible. For example: "When would you like the screen time? Before dinner or after dinner? Saved up for weekends?" "What will help you turn off the TV so that I don't have to ask?"

State the agreement. "OK, our agreement is that you can watch twenty minutes of TV after playing outside. We'll set a timer, and you'll turn off the TV yourself. If I have to ask, you'll skip a day, then try again." End on your child's side, Blackard says, with success in mind: "Show me what it looks like to jump up and turn off the TV so you can watch it the next day."

TRY THIS

How consistent are you really? Step back and consider, from your child's perspective, what message he might be getting from your actions—not just your words.

Emotion first.
Problem second.

....

"I want my mommy. I want my daddy," our friends' 2-year-old sobbed over and over.

We were babysitting him overnight, and he was distraught. We tried distracting him with stories. We sang songs. We tried food. Hugs. Walks. Long, reasoned explanations about how his parents were at a concert, but they were coming back tomorrow—promise. Nothing worked.

Later, we realized he couldn't even hear us: he'd flipped his lid.

That's what Dan Siegel, clinical professor of psychiatry at the UCLA School of Medicine, calls it. He has a great way of explaining how intense emotions shut down the brain's ability to reason:

1. **Hold up your hand.** You're going to make a model of the brain.
2. **Press your thumb to your palm.** The thumb is the limbic area, that ancient part of the brain that regulates emotions. It works in concert with the brain stem (the palm) to signal the rest of your body, including your heart rate and blood pressure.
3. **Wrap your fingers around your thumb.** Your fingers are the cortex, which allows thinking, reasoning, empathy, self-understanding, insight, and balance. Your fingertips are the prefrontal cortex, which is like a lid over the limbic area, keeping emotions in check.
4. **Now pop your fingers back up.** The prefrontal cortex has lost control, because in an emotional situation, the limbic area fires so strongly and repeatedly that it begins overriding the control of the prefrontal cortex. You're no longer able to reason or empathize or otherwise use that higher part of the brain. You've flipped your lid.

That's why it's completely pointless to reason with someone whose emotions are running high, like we tried to do with our friends' 2-year-old that night. And even though my husband and I know about emotion coaching, we'd forgotten about it in our increasing desperation: we'd flipped our lids, too.

This stuff takes practice.

You can see it coming

Now that you can visualize what's happening in the brain, you might start to recognize it: *I'm about to flip my lid,* or *I've already flipped; I need a break.* And you can see it happening in your kids, like when they throw a tantrum or hit.

"We often think that our child needs to learn a lesson here," says parent coach Sarina Natkin, "and we need to teach that lesson immediately."

But a kid can't learn anything when he's flipped his lid. That's why, in the face of intense emotions, it's more productive to:

Acknowledge the emotions first. Label intense feelings (see next page) with empathy.

Deal with the underlying problem second (see page 176).

TRY THIS

Teach the hand model to your 5-year-old, and she might start to tell you when she needs a break. (And probably when you need one, too.)

Label intense emotions

Brain-imaging research shows that verbally naming an intense emotion calms you down. "Name it to tame it," as UCLA psychiatry professor Dan Siegel puts it.

When we babysat our friends' 2-year-old, and he started sobbing about wanting to go home, we tried all sorts of distractions. But we should have gone straight to the emotion, with empathy, for as long as it took to calm him down:

"Oh, sweetie. You want your mommy and daddy. You're feeling so sad right now. It's so nice when your mommy and daddy are here."

The next time we watched him, I just held him, rocked him and patted his back as he sobbed for his mommy and daddy. He didn't name his emotion, but he heard me gently do it for him. He calmed down in less than ten minutes—then fell asleep in my arms.

What I was essentially doing was helping him cry, instead of trying to stop it. Crying is the body's natural way of releasing stress. When we help our children have their emotions in a safe way, we're modeling how to sit with tough emotions, instead of burying them. Why does this matter so much? When emotions aren't released, they get acted out in unpleasant ways. Allowing the emotions is what fully releases them.

Children who can name their own feelings are able to reflect on their feelings, discuss them, decide how to deal with them, recognize feelings in others, and empathize. They tolerate frustration better and get into fewer fights, numerous studies show. They're healthier and less lonely, as well as less impulsive and more focused—which helps them achieve more academically.

For you to be able to name your child's emotion, you need to do a couple things:

Be aware of feelings—your own and others'. Practice by naming your feelings as you go about your day: "I'm feeling anger." "That's frustration." Stating feelings as observations ("I notice I'm feeling sad. I feel a little knot in my throat"), rather than as character traits ("I'm sad"), gives you a little distance from them.

Be accepting of all feelings. Maybe your impulsive response to your friends' 2-year-old would be, "You can go home when your parents get back. For now, let's be happy and play." Or "Big boys don't cry." Or "Your parents aren't here! So enough. Quit crying." None of these responses acknowledge the validity of the emotion.

Being dismissive of certain feelings has roots in the way we were raised. But we can try not to pass that on to our children. Study after study shows the importance of accepting and addressing emotions, no matter how uncomfortable that may be for us.

Technically, some scientists would say emotions are just the brain's way of tagging an event as "very important." Abstractly, emotions just *are*. As you know, no amount of burying or judging or wishing can make them go away.

Might as well accept them.

≫

≪

Ways to help your child identify emotions

- Read stories where the characters deal with feelings. Talk about a time when your child felt that way.
- Put up pictures showing different emotions (pictures you took, or cut from magazines, or bought as a set). When your child is emotional, present the pictures (or look in the mirror): "Here's a sad baby. He's crying. Looks like you feel sad, too." (Avoid questions during intense emotions.)
- Help your child reenact a distressing event using stuffed animals. (Also see Garry Landreth's work on play therapy.)
- Look for a day care or school that practices emotion coaching.
- With school-age children, check out the "Zones of Regulation," which is a sort of emotional thermometer. There's the blue zone (tired, sad), green zone (calm, happy), yellow zone (frustrated, excited), and red zone (angry, out of control). Occasionally ask or note which zone your child is in. It helps her get used to checking in on her own.
- Do a "body check." "Your shoulders are hunched and your fists are clenched, so it looks like you're feeling frustrated right now."

Practice now, while the stakes are low

Why start when kids are young? Because kids are so in tune with their bodies, and emotions live in our bodies. Because *we* need to get used to allowing emotions if we were taught to shut 'em down. And because learning to manage tough emotions takes so much practice.

We want our children to have this skill in place later in life, when the stakes are higher: for being excluded from the group, for that first heartbreak, for not making the team, for dealing with the stresses of college, for managing frustrations at the office, for making a marriage work.

Kids erupt over things that seem ridiculous to adults. But saying, "Oh, you're OK" is dismissive, and even more upsetting. You wouldn't want to hear that if you were angry, right? Acknowledging intense emotions usually helps kids calm themselves enough to turn things around:

"You're feeling mad. You don't want to wear these socks. You're saying, 'No socks!' And it's cold. Cold out, socks on: that's just how it is. Darn it! Must be some place to put these socks. [Playful] On my hands? On your nose? No? Show me where . . ."

"Looks like you feel frustrated! It's frustrating when you want a snack now and can't have it. Show me frustrated. Ooooh. Arms crossed, foot stomping! That's really frustrated! Hmm. Must be something you can do to help you wait..."

If your child gets angry when you start with emotions, start with what your child wants. Identify the emotion afterward.

Say what you see

Handling misbehavior well? It's the toughest thing we parents do. Here are three simple, magical steps to positive parenting.

How do you react when your kid does ____ (thing that upsets you)? What do you say? How do you communicate in a positive way, one that helps your children learn to solve problems, and gives your children a strong sense of who they are? Without having to give it too much thought in the moment? I haven't come across a more powerful strategy than Sandy Blackard's Language of Listening® (languageoflistening.com).

It has only three steps:

1. **Say what you see.**®
2. If you see something you don't like, **offer a can-do**.
3. If you see something you like, **name a strength**.

Say what you see.
Say what your child is doing, saying, feeling, or thinking. Say it without judgment, in a tone that matches your child's energy.

This acknowledgment is a huge relief, brain-imaging studies show, to your child's nervous system. It also gives you a moment to calm down, unflip your lid, and get into the present moment.

Focus on what you actually SEE happening right now—not what you predict about it or how you want to change it or the lesson you've been trying to teach about it. So *Say what you see* is not "You're going to fall" but "You want to climb so high." It's not "Come on, it'll be fun to play with them" but "You want to watch until you feel ready to play." It's not "OK, you're being too loud" but "You want to be loud!" Not "Oh, you're fine" but "You're feeling hurt." Not "We don't grab toys" but "You really want that truck." Not "Hey, I'm trying to talk to you and you're running away" but "You don't want to talk to me right now."

Not "You know better" but "You didn't mean to do that." Not "You're making a mess" but "You want to pour."

When your child is doing something you'd rather he didn't, the easiest place to start is often:

"You want ____."

If you see something you don't like, offer a can-do
Say what your child can do instead. Something that meets their current need and is OK with you.

"You want to jump! You can jump on the floor or you can jump outside." ("You can play with this toy over here" wouldn't meet the need for something physical, right?)

Before age 3, you may want to add a boundary before the can-do. This is useful for defining the problem that needs solving.

"You want to stand. Chairs are for sitting; floors are for standing. You can sit on your chair or stand on the floor."

By age 3, though, your child knows your boundaries; repeating them or focusing on them is just needless lecturing.

≫

«

. . . or let your child find a can-do.

With children age 2 or older, as you both get used to this way of communicating, turn the problem solving over to your child.

[The expression on your face reminds your child the couch isn't for jumping.] "You want to jump! Hmm. Must be something you can do."

You'll be surprised at the solutions kids come up with themselves.

If you see something you like, name a strength.

"You found a fun way to jump on the floor. You're a creative problem-solver."

Here you are shaping who your child believes he is. The proof is right there before both of your eyes: Your child is kind, knowledgeable, generous, compassionate, proud, helpful, assertive, strategic, curious, creative, flexible, able to figure things out, and more. Children already have every possible inner strength, Blackard says. We don't have to teach them those things. We need only point them out as they appear. Isn't that lovely?

Sometimes, though, looking for a strength takes creativity. Did your preschooler just storm off after a friend wouldn't share a toy? Excellent: he's choosing to walk away without hurting his friend. Is your kindergartener having a ball spraying the bathroom mirror with a water bottle? Hmm, actually, that's a pretty good place to do such a thing. Did your toddler decline the eggplant at dinner? OK, she knows what she likes. Or maybe you just don't see a strength right now. You can mention one later or try again next time.

When you do name a strength, try leaving off "I like the way you . . ." Stick with pure acknowledgment, not your approval or disapproval (see page 62). That makes it your child's moment instead of your own.

How do we know what our child wants?

Blackard says children's behavior is driven by three healthy needs:

- Connection
- Experience
- Power

Everything children do is meeting a need they have. This is an incredibly useful lens for looking at our children's actions and words. **Which need is my child meeting right now?** Now we're getting somewhere useful.

Language of Listening is so effective, Blackard theorizes, because it meets all three of our children's needs. Saying what you see creates connection. The can-do provides experience. Naming a strength empowers children.

What else do you notice about this novel way of communicating? You probably notice there are no bribes, rewards, threats, shame, guilt, or even consequences in there. Will you ever use those things? Almost certainly—including the ones you swore you wouldn't. Note how they feel compared to Language of Listening.

For more examples, check out Blackard's book, *Say What You See for Parents and Teachers*, or her online courses at languageoflistening.com.

Guide instead of punish

I assumed it would be a few years before I'd have to think about discipline with my sweet little baby. Nope.

She wasn't a year old before she started doing things I'd just told her not to—and then grinning about it!

My painful introduction to this came during breastfeeding. My baby, apparently testing out her sharp new teeth, started clamping down and then pulling off. I tried showing her my tears. "That really hurts mama!" I said sadly. She had no empathy. I tried biting her shoulder. She screamed; I felt *horrible*. I tried brief time-outs: setting her down next to me on the bed and closing up shop. That didn't quite work, since she was usually still hungry.

Finally, I tried teaching her what *to* do. We were using sign language at the time (see page 68), so she knew the concept of "gentle," which is signed by softly brushing the palm of one hand against the back of the other. We also had played "Say aah!," taking turns opening our mouths wide.

So the next time I (reluctantly) went to nurse her, I said, "Gentle, please. No biting Mommy. When you're done, just open your mouth. Like this." If she did, I exclaimed: "THANK YOU, sweetie! You opened your mouth. Good gentle!" If she bit me, I called a brief time-out. And it worked.

It's not enough to discourage the bad behavior, as I learned. You also have to replace it by teaching the behavior you do want.

I learned this lesson again around 2 years old, when my toddler suddenly started slapping me. My impulse was to gasp in betrayal, grab her wrist, and command, "No hitting!" How effective was that? As soon as I let go, she'd slap me again.

What did work was to say, "We don't hit people. You can hit pillows." Or I'd lightly brush her arm and say, "Hands are for touching gently." She'd then try out the suggestion. "Oh, *thank* you!" I'd gush if she rubbed my arm. "Mommies love massages!"

I also had to learn to look beneath the behavior. (Hmm, I'm trying to catch a break from her. She needs me. Her other ways of saying so didn't work. She hit me. What she really wants is my attention.)

At 3 years old, I am pulling out *all* the tools in my toolbox. I'm also having to face my own subconscious assumptions—like that when my child misbehaves, it's because she *wants* to. I like this line: "Our children aren't giving us a hard time. They're telling us they're having a hard time."

I'm especially grateful to have discovered Sandy Blackard's Language of Listening, the simple framework detailed on page 176.

≫

«

Guidance vs. punishment

We want our children, of course, to know what is acceptable behavior and unacceptable behavior. Some parents think of punishment as the best way to accomplish that. We may yell ("Get over here!") or threaten ("Right now or it's time-out") or bribe ("Eat the broccoli and you can have the ice cream") or shut down emotions ("Don't come to me with that crying") or get more physical than we'd like. And kids may do what we want . . . in the short term. So it looks like it works. We definitely want to do what works!

But punishment doesn't feel very good—to our kids or to us. It is actually less effective in the long term, studies show, for several important reasons:

- children begin to focus on avoiding getting caught, rather than avoiding the bad behavior;
- children from authoritarian homes don't fare as well as children from authoritative homes (see page 160);
- people who are shamed are less likely to take personal responsibility;
- humiliation can lead to rage; and
- correction not directly related to the misbehavior isn't as effective at helping children develop morals.

Isn't punishment an important part of guidance, though—a strong and unmistakable way to teach lessons, instill values, and prove which behavior is acceptable and unacceptable? No. It took me a minute to wrap my mind around this.

Punishment employs shame, guilt, fear, and sometimes physical force. The punishment tends not to relate directly to the misbehavior (taking away dessert, say, for flipping a spoonful of soup). Parents' underlying beliefs are that their children are worthy of respect only when they obey, and that children are motivated to do better only by the fear of punishment. That's an authoritarian parenting style: firm without warmth.

Guidance is focused on helping a child develop self-control, emotional awareness, and problem-solving skills. The child is treated with respect and given the opportunity to solve the problem and make amends (having your child clean up the mess, say, for flipping a spoonful of soup). Parents work to notice acceptable behavior and name their children's strengths. That helps children do it on their own next time.

Parents recognize that a strong relationship with their children, one based on mutual respect and not fear, is the best form of influence they have . . . especially in the teenage years. The underlying belief is that children, with reflection and practice, want to do better. It's an authoritative parenting style: firm and warm.

Guess which is which:

1. "Don't you dare throw toys. Look what you've done! Go to your room and stay there until I say you can come out."
2. "You want to throw. Throwing blocks can hurt people, and that's not OK. Hmm. Must be something you can throw. Yes, a ball! You solved the problem!"

Think back to the kind of person you hope your baby will be as an adult (see page 30). Now consider that imitation is one of the most powerful ways children learn. What parents are modeling through punishment is how to deal with strong emotions by losing self-control. How to communicate disrespectfully. That physical force is a way to solve problems.

Most of us hope to model the opposite: how to control impulses. How to be respectful. How to solve problems without hurting others.

What a huge gap.

If you decide to guide instead of punish, your child is more likely to

- avoid getting into power struggles with you;
- understand that we can control our actions, even if we can't control our emotions; and
- learn the communication, self-control, and problem-solving skills essential for a successful life.

≫

«

Pick up on cues, send cues

Before they act, children send a signal. Maybe your baby gets mad and makes a face: she's about to bite. Maybe your kindergartener comes toward you with tea and a big smile: she wants to share.

When you read your child's signals and respond, you can head off behavior you don't want—or make a sweet moment sweeter. Perhaps you reach for your child with your own big smile. Or you cluck with a soft "No, no, that's not safe."

When your 9-month-old falls, notice the difference between getting anxious (rushing over with "You're OK! You're OK!") and staying calm (making reassuring sounds).

You increase or decrease the intensity of your child's emotion. It's something you do all the time without thinking about it. But it's also a superpower you can use to guide behavior.

Go slow, volume low

Pay attention to your

- **voice**: normal or quieter volume, soothing tone, slower speed
- **actions**: use very slow movements and gestures
- **touch**: loving, gentle, supporting hands
- **proximity**: move close from across the room; get down at eye level

Other cues that can give your child a chance to regain self-control:

- ignore a small misdeed: keep your posture and expression neutral, without eye contact;
- give a stern look;
- make a gesture ("Shh");
- say your child's name;
- give a one-word reminder ("Gently").

Why don't kids just follow the rules?

At some point, kids know they shouldn't hit or shove or snatch away toys.

If you ask them, they will tell you it's wrong. But in the heat of the moment, they hit. What to do instead hasn't yet become second nature. Knowledge becomes second nature only through repeated action. Through repeated action, knowledge is passed from the prefrontal cortex, where we do our logical thinking, to the subcortical regions of the brain, where actions are automatic.

Kids need to repeat the *action*. That's why lecturing isn't very effective. ("How many times do I have to tell you . . . ?") Instead, try, "Let's have a do-over." Literally return things to their previous state and start again. Model with your child what you would like to happen. Or help your child succeed by providing hints and prompts—a strategy called "scaffolding." For example, in some classrooms, children are given a drawing of an ear to hold when they should be listening and a drawing of a mouth when it's their turn to talk. Over time, as you notice your children growing in their abilities, you gradually reduce the scaffolding.

A little empathy and a lot of patience never hurt, either.

TRY THIS

The Wheel of Choice

When your child gets angry and acts out, one goal is to help him understand that, while he can't choose his emotions, he can choose his behavior. Enter the Wheel of Choice. It's an illustrated pie chart you make with your child (not foisted on your child), from positive-discipline pioneer Jane Nelsen.

A Wheel of Choice might have options like "Tell them to stop," "Count to ten," "Tell them how I feel," "Walk away," "Punch a pillow," "Save for family meeting" (see page 144), and "Apologize." When your child gets angry, point him to the Wheel of Choice.

Ways to respond that guide instead of punish

WHEN YOUR CHILD HURTS OTHERS

Say what you see. "You got mad and you hit me. You want some mama time and, oh no, I need quiet time."

Offer a can-do. "Must be something you can do to help you wait."

Name a strength. "You figured out a solution! You'll set up a game for us and come get me when the timer goes off!"

Say what you see. "You bit your cousin! Now he is crying."

Offer a can-do. "Must be something you can do to help him feel better."

Name a strength. "You asked if he is OK. You know how to make it right."

Say what you see. "You both really want that toy and, aghh, there's only one!"

Offer a can-do. "Must be something that will work for both of you."

Or "You can tell her you like her toy and ask her when you can hold it."

Name a strength. "You waited, she shared, and now you are both happy."

Or "She didn't want to share, and you respected that."

Or "You got mad that she didn't want to share, and you turned away. That shows you have self-control."

WHEN YOUR CHILD ACTS UP IN PUBLIC

"This isn't working for me. We're leaving the store now. Do you want to walk, be carried, or have a piggyback ride?"

Say what you see. "You don't like the soup."

State a firm boundary + can-do. "That kind of talk is not OK with me. Instead of 'I hate this soup!' it would be more considerate to say, 'I'm not wild about this soup.'" (This was my mom's preferred phrase when we didn't like her cooking.)

Name a strength. "That was considerate."

⋯⋯⋯⋯⋯⋯⋯⋯⋯⋯⋯⋯⋯⋯⋯⋯⋯⋯

Say what you see. "You want to tell me something."

Offer a can-do. "Mean words make it hard for me to hear. Tell me in more respectful words."

Name a strength. "I heard you that time. You spoke respectfully."

Say what you see. "You wish we could read right now, just you and me . . ."

State a firm boundary + can-do. ". . . and I have to nurse the baby. The hard part is waiting. Must be something you can do."

Or ". . . and I have to nurse the baby. You can set the timer, and then we can read."

Name a strength. "You waited as long as you could."

⋯⋯⋯⋯⋯⋯⋯⋯⋯⋯⋯⋯⋯⋯⋯⋯⋯⋯

Say what you see. "Your sister wants to play, and you want to be left alone."

Offer a can-do. "I wonder if someone has an idea."

Name a strength. "You figured out how to play together."

Ways to respond that guide instead of punish

Many of these examples were quick and smooth. How might this play out in real life as you stumble along through it? If you hit resistance at any point, you circle back to the top. See if you can pick out the various rounds of Say What You See, Can-Dos, and Strengths.

Me: We need to detangle your hair before ballet.

G, *who hates having her hair combed:* Why-y-y?

Me: Miss Darien expects your hair up. *(OK, I made that up.)* Let's get your hair wet in the sink.

G: Running away!

G runs off and pretends to bake cookies.

Me, *considering picking her up off the ground but instead committing to do this:* You want to make cookies, and your hair needs to be detangled for ballet. Hmm. Must be something you can do.

Long silence. G begins to play with another game, but slowly.

Me: You're opening your GoldieBlox box. You're closing your GoldieBlox box. Your back is turned. You're thinking about it.

G turns to me with a big grin.

Me: There's my ballerina!

G, *brightly:* I have an idea!

Me: What's that?

G: I'll play GoldieBlox until the cookies are ready.

Me, *hoping for more*: Mm-hmm?

G: And then we'll detangle my hair.

Me, *kind of amazed*: You have a plan!

G: Mm-hmm!

Me: Let me know when you're ready. (*I should have said, "How many minutes until cookies are ready?"*)

Me, *10 minutes later, realizing that was too open-ended*: Little G, we have one more minute before we detangle your hair.

G: Mom, I have a lot more pages to do.

Me: You want to look at your pages, and we need to detangle your hair. Hmm. Must be something you can do.

G: I'm turning my body away.

Me, *starting to feel desperate*: You're turning your body away and we're running out of time.

Long pause.

G: The detangle game! (*Now she's the one making things up.*)

Me, *even more amazed*: The detangle game! Who can get to the bathroom first?

We race there, comb her curls with the usual tears and empathy, and leave for ballet.

Me: That was hard, but you did it.

G: I did it.

More ways to respond that guide instead of punish

....

Lying is actually a sign that your child's "theory of mind," the ability to guess others' thoughts and motivations, is developing properly. Children enter this stage around age 2. Children at this age also are incredibly imaginative, not entirely clear on what is real and what is imagined, and testing out the bound-aries of fantasy vs. reality through storytelling. They say things they wish to be true. They claim things are the opposite of what you see in front of your eyes.

It's not useful to get upset about untruths at this stage, even though the lies seem to be insulting your intelligence: "I'm not drinking cranberry juice in the living room." Respond matter-of-factly: "Sounds like you know the rule. Now, show me where you can drink juice."

When kids pretend or exaggerate, play along. "I made the sky." "That must have been a lot of work. Look at all that blue!"

"The tiger did it." "Ah. I'd like you to help your tiger clean up this spill."

"It was the baby!" "I know you *wish* your sister did this, but I know it was you. Please help me put this plant back in the pot."

By age 4, children know the difference between telling the truth and lying. When you notice it, let them know: "Hmm. That's not true. For some reason you don't feel like you can tell me the truth, even though you know you feel better when you do," parenting coach Sandy Blackard suggests saying. "We need to talk about this." Also notice when they tell the truth: "Even though that was difficult, you told the truth. That tells me you are honest."

But first, avoid putting your kids in a tough position by

making statements . . .	instead of asking questions
"Looks like the painting has been splattered with sauce. Tell me about that."	"Who did this to my painting?!"
"I see you have one of your friend's toys. We'll need to take that back."	"Did you steal this toy?!"
"I saw you break the cabinet door. I need you to tell me when something like that happens, so we can fix it."	"Why didn't you tell me you broke the cabinet door?"
"I see you didn't clean your room / do your homework. What do you need to be able to start?"	"Did you clean your room / do your homework?"

Then give your child a chance to make it right. For example, have your child help clean up the mess, fix a broken item, or tell a friend she took a toy.

WHEN YOUR CHILD WON'T LISTEN

Sometimes we just talk too much.

My daughter's shorts got muddy (we were camping), and I'd encouraged her to wash them in the water spigot (an object of immense fascination). As she began, I could tell she needed to pee. Like many kids, she'll do a potty dance 'til the cows come home before admitting she has to go.

"Sweetie, why don't you go to the bathroom," I said. "You can wash your shorts after that."

She continued washing her shorts. Meanwhile, she was doing that butt-way-back marching-slowly-in-place crouch thing.

"I can see you need to go potty," I said. "Let's go to the bathroom—it's right here. And then we'll come back to finish washing your shorts."

She continued washing her shorts.

"Little G!" I said, coming closer. "Potty first. Shorts later."

"OH!" she exclaimed, as though suddenly enlightened. "Potty first! Shorts later!"

And she happily ran off to the bathroom.

What the...? I thought. Later I realized "Talk to your baby a ton" (see page 52) is a concept I'd taken too far. That tip is actually about creating a conversation with your baby about the world she's encountering. It doesn't refer to making requests. And it doesn't excuse a bunch of filler words.

Well, my daughter just schooled me on filler words. Lesson learned.

"Come on, you need to get dressed right *now*! We are out of time! Put on these pants!" I said in frustration, for what felt like the sixth time, as my daughter ran around doing ballet moves. I wised up. Say what you see.

"You want to be a ballerina!" I held her pants open and playfully directed a can-do. "The ballerina dances into her pants! She points her right toes and ... in. She points her left toes and ... in." There. Pants on. With smiles.

I know I've sometimes felt like I'd be rewarding bad behavior with my attention or good mood. (Even if I've contributed to the behavior by calling out commands over my shoulder instead of coming close and helping.) And it can be hard to suddenly conjure up a playful attitude when I'm feeling frustrated. But the alternative, continuing down a bad path, is worse.

Playfulness truly—and instantly—turns things around. For both parties.

Me: Are you done? Bring your bowl to the kitchen.

G: I don't want to.

Me: Well, we need to bring our bowls inside.

G: No. I won't.

Me, *wanting to say "Yes, you will" but predicting how that will play out, so switching to Language of Listening:*

Say what you see. You want to leave your bowl out on the deck.

Let your child find a can-do. What might happen to it out there?

G: The wind might blow it away.

Me: Oh no! You wouldn't want that to happen to your favorite bowl.

G, *happily bringing bowl inside*: No, I wouldn't!

Name a strength: You know where things go.

Plan ahead to avoid trouble

What's better than a pound of punishment? As many ounces of prevention as possible.

Set your children up for success. Are they rested and fed at the moment? Have they gotten out to run and play? Have they had a few recent minutes of one-on-one time, where you've given them your full attention? If not, it's going to be hard for them to self-regulate or to focus on much else. So that's not the time to go shopping, look at your phone, or attempt a conversation with another adult. Recognize when you've pushed it too far. When they inevitably misbehave—crying, whining, hitting, throwing things, running around maniacally—the kindest response is not discipline but supplying the missing ingredient. Have snacks and water on hand. Plan breaks in a place where your child can race around. Ease the transitions between activities.

For example, give five minutes of advance notice (at home, singing the same song is a great cue) and allow unhurried time to say "Bye-bye, toys" when it's time to clean up and go.

Give smiles, hugs, and choices. Children seek control, because who wants their every move to be managed by someone else? And they seek the attention they need from you. Giving both control and attention in positive ways reduces the likelihood that children will seek them in negative ways.

Really be present with your child for a time each day. Create moments of positive attention, like a wink, smile, or hug. Notice and point out behavior you like.

Offer small choices to give your child more control over his day, such as which shirt to wear, using this cup or that one, or which books to read. Even when there's no real choice, you can create one: "Would you like to put on your shoes, or would you like me to help you?"

Explain what's about to happen. Setting expectations is one of the most useful things my husband and I have gotten into the habit of doing with baby. "We're going to sit on the potty, and then we'll play with the blocks. First potty, then play." "This is our last bedtime story. After this story, I'm going to say good night and close the door . . . OK, that was our last story. Now I'm going to leave and close the door. Good night, beautiful baby."

Say yes instead of no. "Yes, it would be nice to . . ." "Yes, I wish we could . . ." "Yes, you can do X after we do Y." "Absolutely, we can do that tomorrow."

Think before you act—or, at least, after. You're going to get caught off guard by your child's misbehavior, and your first reaction may or may not be what you'd like. But later, when you're calm, take the time to plan out a better response. Your plan might not go perfectly, but hey, you'll have plenty of chances to practice it. You can always say, "I wish I'd handled that differently. Can I have a do-over?"

≫

DINNERTIME! WHAT'S TAKING YOU GUYS SO LONG?

Our toddler suddenly refused to sit in her high chair during meals. She wanted to sit in our laps, take one bite, and go play. Trying to get some food in her, we found ourselves kind of chasing her around with a forkful of dinner.

Stepping back, we came up with a plan. Instead of trying to get her in the high chair first, we sat down and started eating our dinner. When she came over, wanting to climb in our laps, we said amenably, "Mommy sits in her chair at dinnertime. Daddy sits in his chair. You sit in your chair." She would protest; we would repeat ourselves and turn back to eating. Soon, she would climb into her high chair.

After a week or two of this routine, with my husband also using it at breakfast, baby no longer protested. Then, to my surprise, one day a few weeks later, she took her plate from the kitchen, set it on the dining room table, moved her chair into place, climbed up into it, buckled herself in, and announced it was dinnertime—before we sat down ourselves.

«

Call a calm-down for yourself. As soon as you realize you're upset, stop. Turn away if needed. Name your emotion: "I'm feeling really frustrated." Take some deep breaths. Wait until you're calm. Then act. (See page 199.)

Remember that you can't control someone else's behavior. This concept has circumvented a lot of frustration for me. Infants are so adoring and compliant that you're a little thrown when your toddler starts up with "*No*, mama! I don't *WANT* it!" The truth is, you can't make your child do anything. And your child doesn't want to do everything you ask just because *you're* the one asking. You can really only tell your kids what you expect and how you will behave. Not how they will behave.

Realizing that I can't *make* baby wear a hat, sit on the potty, or eat more dinner reduces tension and potential power struggles around those daily things. It gives my child space to show her likes and dislikes. It gives me space to notice those things and accept who she is, instead of overriding them with who I am.

I might want to say, "It's cold outside, so yes, you will wear a hat." Instead I say, "I will bring your hat in case you change your mind." It might seem faster to threaten: "Do it on the count of three, or I will." Instead, I dig for patience. "I'm ready to move on. I will take two deep breaths, and then I will help you." I might prefer to say, "You hardly ate anything. Just take three more bites." I hold my tongue. "If you're hungry, now is the time to eat. I'm clearing the table soon. I will make a snack later."

Take the long view. If only children learned self-discipline—or anything else—in just one sitting. We parents have at least twenty years to teach this stuff to our kids—and even then the brain isn't finished developing. So when your kid fails to clean his room for the third time, maybe it's OK to say, "I think we're both really tired right now. Tomorrow let's talk and come up with a plan for keeping your room clean."

Rock your routines

Every day, my husband wakes up at the same time, pushes the jogging stroller along the same route, feeds our baby oatmeal for breakfast, and makes a ham sandwich for lunch.

Me, I'm all over the place. I might go to bed at 10:00 p.m. or 2:00 a.m. I might get wrapped up in a project and forget to eat lunch. But I know babies thrive on routine, so I work hard to keep our baby's meals and naps on a regular schedule. Her babysitters come on the same days each week. She goes to bed at about the same time each night, because we don't plan outings that conflict.

Research shows we're on the right track. Routines help kids:

- plan and make predictions about the future, helping to develop executive function.
- feel independent, because they're able to do part of a task themselves after practicing it over and over.
- practice self-control (see page 116).

For babies, routine means creating structure with consistent meal times, sleep times, and bedtime routines. After age 3 or so, you can help your kids create and follow their own routines. A checklist is one good way to start.

The checklist

Create a morning checklist together, written or just illustrated, of everything the kids need to do before school.

List no more than seven tasks. A 3-year-old might have only a few: go potty, eat breakfast, get dressed. A 5-year-old's list would include more tasks: get dressed, make bed, make lunch, eat breakfast, brush teeth, and put on shoes, coat, and backpack. Prompt your child to come up with the items: "And what will you need for walking outside?"

≫

≪

As the kids get distracted during their morning routine, remind them: "Check the list." That's it. Instead of yelling, "Did you brush your teeth? I told you ten minutes ago to brush your teeth! Where are your shoes?!" you can simply say, as many times as is needed: "What do you need to be doing right now? Check the list."

Point out your kids' successes throughout the morning. "You checked the list. Now I smell minty fresh breath! Can I have a minty fresh kiss?" Within a few weeks of practice, kids start checking the list on their own. Mornings, parents report, look a lot less like mutiny.

Call a calm-down, not a time-out

Typical time-outs are carried out so ineffectively, it's better to just rename them.

What parents usually do is threaten a time-out, lecture, threaten again, finally send their child away, angrily wrestle their child back into the time-out spot a few times, yell at them to be quiet if they sound like they're having fun in there, fret over them if they're crying, make their child apologize afterward, and wrap up with a lecture. In other words, a heck of a lot of attention.

The truly effective technique? Briefly *withdrawing* attention from your child's misbehavior.

You go first:

"I need to calm down. I'm going to read in my room for a few minutes."

"Time for a calm-down. I'm going to take deep breaths."

"We're not going to talk about this until we're both calm."

Calm-downs are used for stopping disruptive or defiant behavior. But think of them as positive, not punitive. Their purpose is to give your child—and you— a moment to stop and regain self-control.

When you're not in the heat of the moment, prepare

Figure out what calms your child. What should your child be doing during a calm-down? Not "thinking about what she just did." That's not gonna happen; emotions are running too high. Instead, she should do an activity that you know tends to calm her.

Together, brainstorm ideas. It could be taking deep breaths (a 2½-year-old or 3-year-old can do this), punching a pillow, jumping up and down, mashing playdough, asking for a hug, looking at a book, listening to soothing music, drawing, stretching, doing windmills or sit-ups or squats, staring out the window . . . Whatever works.

≫

«

Create a Wheel of Choice. Write the ideas on a pie chart, illustrating each item with a drawing or photo. Role-play each one, suggests parent coach Sarina Natkin, so your child is clear about what they mean. Pretend to be mad, go over to the Wheel of Choice, pick an option, and do that thing. Kids usually find this hilarious.

Choose a calm-down space. This could be a corner of the house or a spot in your child's room—a place your child chooses for herself. Make it cozy. Make it a place your child wants to go even when it's not time to cool off.

WHY TYPICAL TIME-OUTS DON'T WORK WELL

Your child is overwhelmed by an intense emotion, which is why she's flipped her lid (see page 170) and acted out. She needs to regain self-control. Sending her to her room as a punishment doesn't teach her how to calm down.

If your child does stay in time-out, she's likely sitting there burning with resentment, not learning how to calm herself. In the end, studies show, she will be more compliant with your commands. But compliance out of fear of punishment isn't a goal of authoritative parents.

A calm-down lets your child practice dealing with intense emotions. This eventually teaches her an alternative to the behavior that led to the calm-down. It teaches her that taking a break when you're worked up is a good thing, not a bad thing.

How to call a calm-down

1. **Keep the conversation short and sweet.** "OK, time for a calm-down." Be matter-of-fact, not threatening or disrespectful.

   It's not necessary to send your child away. (The key is withdrawing attention from the misbehavior, not the child.) You might say, "Would you like to sit next to me while you calm down?"

   Or "Would you like to go to your calm-down space, or should I go to mine?" If your child won't choose, parent coach Sarina Natkin says, announce your own plan for calming down: "I'm going to ___." You might add, "I love you, but I'm too worked up (or I've flipped my lid, or I'm in the yellow zone) and can't talk about this right now."

   In some cases, say nothing at all. If you've told your children you will ignore any bickering, simply don't respond to bickering. If you've told your children you'll pull over the car whenever they argue in the backseat, simply pull over. As soon as the misbehavior stops (give it thirty seconds to make sure), carry on.

2. **Practice a calming technique.** This does three things: It models for your child how to calm down. It calms you down. And it withdraws your attention from your child's misbehavior.

   You could take deep breaths, sit down with a book or your phone (even if you're too worked up to concentrate at first), or pick something from your child's Wheel of Choice.

   Depending on the situation, you might do these alone, your child might do them alone, or you might do them together. Some parents ask if their children would like a hug first.

3. **Point out successes.** "You calmed yourself!"

4. **Later, teach the lesson.** Once everyone is calm, or even that evening, talk with your child about both the misbehavior (including your child's intentions) and the desired behavior. Ask questions in a nonjudgmental way: "What happened there?" "What can you do differently next time?" "What do we need to do to make this right?"

Ask, "Can you think of a better way?"

The best criticism gives constructive feedback or encourages problem-solving.

In one study, kindergarteners were given a scenario: a teacher asks them to create a house out of Legos, and they forget to put in windows. Then the teacher and child role-play what happens next, using dolls and speaking for them. (Researchers sometimes use this approach because young children readily imagine and insert themselves into role-playing scenarios.) Playing the part of her doll, the teacher says, "The house has no windows," and gives one of the following three criticisms.

Character judgment: "I'm disappointed in you."

Constructive feedback: "That's not the right way to do it, because the blocks are not straightened up and are still messy."

Encouraging problem-solving: "Maybe you could think of another way to do it."

Researchers, led by Melissa Kamins and Carol Dweck at Columbia University, then assessed the children's feelings of self-worth: the extent to which the children felt smart, good, nice, and competent. The children rated their mood, and rated the house as a product.

Criticizing character hurts self-worth, mood, persistence
Children whose character was criticized rated themselves lower in self-worth, had a more negative mood, were less persistent, and were more likely to view this one instance of less-than-stellar performance as a reflection of their character.

Children encouraged to solve the problem themselves had far more positive ratings in every category, while the ratings by children given constructive feedback about the outcome landed somewhere in the middle.

The children were asked to keep role-playing: "What happens next?" The answers of the children given character criticism are a little bit heartbreaking:

"She should cry and go to bed." "The teacher got mad and went home."

"He should get a time-out."

The answers of the children encouraged to problem-solve: "I can do it again better if I take my time." "I'll take it apart and put it together again with windows."

"I would say it's not finished yet, then I could cut out squares from paper and paste them onto the house."

TRY THIS

Here are a few ways to encourage problem-solving:

- *"What do you think happened here?"*
- *"What could you do differently next time?"*
- *"Can you think of a better way to do it?"*

GOOD TO KNOW

Dweck cautions against protecting children from criticism. "Constructive criticism discusses with kids what they did wrong, why they did it wrong, and what they can do better next time. Kids cannot learn without criticism," she says. "And if you never criticize them, they will think mistakes are so terrible that they can't confront them."

Move

Our bodies and brains crave movement. But if it was tough to fit in a workout before baby, try after. So now is a good time to multitask. Lifting baby is exercise, right? Can you get places you need to go, but without the car?

Rock, jiggle, and swing

Babies crave motion so much, they go through a phase of doing it themselves: bouncing, swaying, rocking, and sometimes (upsettingly) head banging.

As it turns out, having a good sense of balance and motion is associated with baby's learning ability. Who would guess?

Scientist Lise Eliot suggests thinking of it this way: our higher-level emotional and cognitive abilities are built on top of a foundation of our sensory and motor abilities.

The part of the body that controls balance and motion, the vestibular system, is found to be lacking among children with emotional problems, attention deficits, learning disabilities, language disorders, and autism.

Motion soothes
Researchers had parents soothe newborns 2 to 4 days old by either holding them or rocking, carrying, and jiggling. The second option worked better.

Playing spin the baby

Sitting in a swivel chair with an infant on their laps, researchers spun around and stopped abruptly, waiting for thirty seconds before spinning again. Babies were held in several positions, to affect the three semicircular ear canals: head tilted forward thirty degrees, side-lying on the right, and side-lying on the left. Researchers did this spinning routine twice a week for a month, ten spins in each position. And? Compared to controls, the babies who spun had better reflexes and were better at sitting, crawling, standing, and walking.

TRY THIS

"Row, Row, Row Your Boat"

Get into airplane position: lay on your back with your knees close to your chest.
Set baby tummy-down on your shins, facing you, and hold baby's hands.

Sing "Row, row, row your boat, gently down the stream . . ."
Raise and lower your feet to move baby up and down

"Merrily, merrily, merrily, merrily . . ."
Swim baby's arms

"Life is but a dream!"
Cup baby's shoulders, one in each hand. Lift your feet up, straightening your legs, so baby is upside down. Lower baby back to the ground to finish.

Keep moving

Exercise does tremendous things for mind, body, and soul.

It boosts problem-solving skill, abstract-thinking ability, long-term memory, reasoning, attention, and more. It reduces anxiety, stress, and depression. How? Exercise

- increases oxygen to the brain,
- helps create and protect neurons,
- elevates a chemical called brain-derived neurotrophic factor (or BDNF) that knocks down a toxic stress hormone, and
- releases chemical messengers (norepinephrine, serotonin, dopamine) that act against mood disorders.

All sorts of things, it turns out, go haywire in the body when you're sedentary.

I thought a sedentary person was someone who lays on the couch all day, eating chips and watching TV. Turns out "sedentary" refers to almost all of us. If you sit for most of the day, like at the office, you're at higher risk for chronic disease—*even if you do a workout at some point.* Excessive sitting has such a detrimental effect on your metabolic rate that Mayo Clinic researcher James Levine calls it a "lethal activity."

Harvard evolutionary biologist Daniel Lieberman estimates that our hunter-gatherer ancestors walked five and a half to nine miles a day. The conditions that forged our brains often are the ones we still thrive in today.

You still want to get vigorous exercise (where you're breathing hard) totaling at least thirty minutes per day. But it's just as important to be moving, not sitting, throughout the day. If you're a stay-at-home parent, you'll probably be grateful for just a moment to sit down and rest. If not, think seriously about ways to wean yourself from your car, your sit-down desk, and your TV.

This concept goes for baby, too. Toddlers need to toddle. Older kids need at least an hour a day of an aerobic activity, like running, jump rope, basketball, swimming, or soccer. Get them moving for at least fifteen minutes of every hour.

THE RESEARCH

Using data from a huge multiyear study on aging, researchers looked at sixty-three thousand men ages 45–64 and found that those who sat more than four hours a day were "significantly more likely" to have been diagnosed with heart disease, cancer, diabetes, or high blood pressure than those who sat less than four hours a day.

TRY THIS

The most useful piece of advice I've gotten from my toddler's pediatrician so far is to make sure she gets enough exercise during the day. If I don't make the effort to get us out of the house—yes, some days that takes effort—I notice that baby gets cranky, has trouble napping, and races around in the evening as if to make up for it. One of the best cures for crankiness seems to be walking outside.

Ideas for exercise

Look for gyms and yoga studios that offer child care (this costs only $3–$5 per session where I live, in Seattle—so worth it). Hopefully a class will land just outside of nap time. If you're a stay-at-home parent, put every option into your calendar so that you know where you can go when the opportunity strikes.

Join a parent-and-baby workout class like Stroller Strides, Strollercize, Stroller Fit, Baby Boot Camp, yoga, or swimming.

Get a jogging stroller so that you can get outside on your own schedule (meaning, on baby's unpredictable schedule).

Find a workout buddy. Ideally, this is someone whose kid takes predictable naps that line up with your kid's naps. Or someone who is flexible enough that you can adjust the timing on the fly, because it's so hard to get out of the house on time with a baby at first. Or someone who can meet you before baby wakes up or while your partner feeds baby breakfast.

Do something you love. If the word "workout" makes you shudder, go hiking or dancing or anything else where breaking a sweat is just a bonus.

DO IT NOW

What will you do to get thirty minutes of vigorous exercise?
Be specific about the days, times, and places.

Ideas for movement

Leave the car at home. Yes, it takes more time to walk the forty minutes to the restaurant than to drive the ten minutes. Is that so bad? You gain time to talk with your lunch date, you feel more connected to your surroundings, and you feel great after your meal. Perhaps a grocery store or farmers' market is within walking distance. You could stuff your purchases in the jogging stroller. Or you could bike for your errands, putting items in a backpack or saddlebag, or tucked around your child in a bike trailer. Even if the place is five miles away, getting there by bicycle will take only thirty minutes or so. Hey, now you've gotten your thirty minutes of vigorous exercise.

The idea that movement is more important than speed definitely takes a shift in thinking. You could work on it incrementally, like walking or biking part of the way, and busing or driving the rest. Or you could make a dramatic change, like choosing a smaller house in a walkable neighborhood over a suburban house where it's impractical to walk or bike.

Are you thinking, "I couldn't do that"?

Take a minute to write out your concerns. Next to each one, brainstorm about what would remove that obstacle. For example, if biking seems impossible because "I don't know how I'd get there," resolve to check a few routes using the biking and bus options built into Google Maps, and begin imagining how it could work.

If it's "I don't like walking in this weather," resolve to buy the right gear, try it, and see if it's as horrible as you imagine. If one benefit of a suburban home is "a safe place for kids to play," your requirement of an urban home could be "on a quiet street near a park."

Dig into the why, and come up with the why not.

≫

«

Stand at your desk. It's hard to get away from sitting eight hours a day if there's a chair at your desk. Fortunately, standing desks no longer seem weird. (Mine involves a laptop on a plastic storage bin, and an external monitor, but there are fancier options.) Treadmill desks aren't far behind; you can even buy them at Target. You walk slowly on them as you work.

Early adopters swear by treadmill desks. There's late-show host Jimmy Kimmel, weatherman Al Roker, and *New Yorker* staff writer Susan Orlean. Orlean told NPR that her afternoon work slump is gone, and she doesn't miss sitting: "The funny thing is that when I leave my office, it's not that I think, 'Oh my God, thank goodness I can finally go sit.' I find that I have more energy, and what often comes to mind is, 'Oh, I think I'll take the dog and go for a walk.'"

And there's "dworley" at instructables.com, who made me laugh: "[A]fter the initial adjustment period, during which walking was torture and standing was something I did for emergencies, I can now say that it's solely responsible for all the happiness I've ever had."

Choose the harder way. Take the stairs instead of the elevator, even if your office is twenty floors up. Carry baby in a wrap or hiking backpack instead of in a stroller. Run with the stroller instead of walk, even for a short stretch. Park as far away as possible. Our natural instinct is to choose the easy way, so we have to consciously override this.

Be a stay-at-home parent. You'll be on your feet all day! Stretching across the kitchen to cook and clean, bending down to pick up toys/baby/spills, wrestling baby into diapers and clothes, taking walks just to get out of the house . . . You'll still need thirty minutes of vigorous exercise, but in my experience, you sure won't be sitting.

(DO IT NOW)

What specific things will you do to keep from sitting for long stretches?

Slow down

Babies are slow. And babies are all-encompassing. The more present you are when you're with baby—leaving work at work, stashing digital distractions, and including baby in the day's tasks (even though they'll take longer)—the more you'll enjoy baby. Embrace baby pace.

Be still

How often do we pause to just *be?*

Studies hint that people who meditate daily have

- more gray matter in parts of the brain associated with memory and learning, and less gray matter in parts of the brain associated with stress.
- more folds, and thus more neurons, in the cerebral cortex. The number of folds increases the more years one has been meditating, proving that brain growth is not on an irreversible decline after one's early 20s, as once thought.
- more empathy. When they hear the sounds of someone suffering, a part of the brain related to empathy reacts more strongly.
- longer attention spans.

The *New York Times* calls meditation "A bench press for the brain." That's because stillness—meditation—is challenging mental work.

Meditation isn't about sitting there with your eyes closed, trying to force your mind not to have thoughts. Instead, you continually bring your awareness back to the present moment, often by focusing your attention on the breath and letting random thoughts float away as they come up. Our minds really like to wander, so it takes work to stay in the present for more than a few seconds.

A mind that's better at focusing is also better at working memory (that's the ability to retain and use bits of information). In one study, researchers asked undergraduates to meditate for two weeks, and found that their working memory improved while their mind wandering decreased. On a GRE test, their average verbal-reasoning scores improved by 13 percent.

For kids, a walking meditation

Children have trouble sitting still for long (if you haven't noticed). But they can meditate by walking silently for five minutes at a time. In Montessori schools, children walk while holding a bell, trying not to let it ring.

After age 10, introduce the concept of sitting comfortably in a quiet place and focusing on the breath. Have your kids put a hand on their belly and notice how it feels to breathe deeply. Teach them to repeat a simple phrase, such as "Love," "Om," or "I am," said with each breath, which helps quiet the mind.

At Nataki Talibah Schoolhouse, a charter school in Detroit, students in fifth to eighth grades meditate by closing their eyes and silently repeating a mantra for ten minutes, twice a day. A study of the children found them to be happier, with higher self-esteem, better able to handle stress, and more socially skilled than children at another Detroit school who didn't meditate.

Something to keep in mind.

Be truly present in the moment

One powerful meditation practice is taking the time to really notice what you're experiencing at the moment.

It could be during a meal: chewing slowly, noticing the texture and tastes in your mouth, listening to the sound your teeth make, noticing what your tongue is doing and what happens in your throat as you swallow. It could be during a meeting: sensing how the muscles in your back and legs continually adjust

≫

as you're sitting. It could be during a hike: pausing in silence until you start to hear the chirps of distant birds, the rush of a stream, the wind rustling leaves, and the other subtle sounds of the forest.

Here's one exercise to help you get the idea, which might work with older kids, too. Find a partner, and sit comfortably close to each other. The first person asks, "What are you experiencing right now?"

The other person responds with whatever sensation or emotion or thought comes to mind. "The sound of birds outside." "Heat spreading across my chest." "A desire to hide."

The first person replies, "Thank you." As in, thank you for being vulnerable in this moment and sharing this thing with me.

Take a breath or two. Repeat the question. Go for five minutes, then switch roles.

Seattle teacher Brent Morton led a group of us through this exercise during a yoga retreat, and the experience stuck with me. A partner helps you stay focused on the meditation, because you know you'll need an answer to the upcoming question. Your answers get deeper as you go on, if you let them, and that vulnerability creates a connection with the other person. It also can be good practice in verbalizing your emotions (see page 180).

TRY THIS

Students (including 5-year-olds) in a traditional Tae Kwon Do class were directed to ask themselves three questions:

1. *Where am I?*

2. *What am I doing?*

3. *What should I be doing?*

The first question brings the student's focus to the present moment. The second question centers the student's mind on a specific, clear goal. The third question helps the student check in to see if his current actions will help him achieve the goal at hand.

I'm putting this tidbit in my back pocket, because these questions seem useful for a kid doing pretty much any activity. Heck, they seem useful for me.

Don't bother to compare

My friend has figured out the correct answer to any baby-related news.

If you tell him your baby is now crawling/sitting/walking/talking/climbing/whatever, he will exclaim: "Al*ready?!?*" It feels good to hear that, right? We all want our babies to be at least a little bit north of average.

The reality: it's pointless to compare kids.

No two brains are the same
Children's brains don't go through developmental phases in the same way, at the same time, or in the same order. They may skip and then circle back to phases. They may repeat some. Even the phases themselves are in dispute. The brain is a mysterious thing.

And since both experiences and genetics wire our brains, it's impossible for any two brains to be the same—including those of identical twins.

Understand age-appropriate behavior

It's still helpful to know what most kids are capable of and when, so that your expectations aren't unrealistic.

Is your 3-month-old not sleeping through the night? Has your 18-month-old started slapping you? Does your 4-year-old seem even less willing to share than before? All normal. (You can sign up at babycenter.com for a weekly e-mail about what babies at a certain age are often up to.)

But the next time you're comparing notes with friends or forums, don't get overly worried or overly proud.

And the next time parents innocently fill you in on a milestone, make 'em feel good. "Al*ready?!?*"

TRY THIS

"Don't bother to compare" goes for parenting, too. We can be so judgmental of others' choices. The authors of I Was a Really Good Mom Before I Had Kids *observe that this comes from a place of insecurity, a need to validate our own parenting choices. We're all doing the best we can, right? We need all the support and encouragement we can get. (If you're feeling the weight of high self-expectations, and you need a laugh, read that book.)*

Find your own work-family balance

A majority of new mothers surveyed say that, for them, working part-time or not at all would be ideal.

Of mothers currently working full-time:	Of mothers currently not working:
44% would rather be working part-time	40% would rather be working part-time
9% would rather stay at home full-time	36% are happy staying at home full-time

Pew Research Center, March 2013

Moms who work part-time for first few years tend to be happier

In a Pew Research Center survey, mothers working part-time up through the preschool years report

- less depression than stay-at-home moms;
- better general health than stay-at-home moms;
- less social isolation, which affects mental health;
- greater ability to develop new skills, which also affects mental health;
- less work-family conflict, compared with women working full-time; and
- more sensitive parenting, compared with women working full-time or staying at home.

Past preschool, the story shifts. At an equal rate, the Pew survey reports, women who work for pay and those who don't report being "very happy" with their lives: 36 percent for both groups. Being married is a stronger predictor of happiness than work status.

This may or may not describe you, of course. It's just food for thought as you figure out what you want to do work-wise. A few potential reasons for the results of the survey:

- Staying at home full-time, parenting for hours on end, is exhausting mental and emotional work. Just from a brain perspective, it involves staying constantly alert, making a staggering number of decisions, rapidly intuiting and responding to another person's needs, and acting with empathy and self-control.
- Working part-time for pay (or studying at school) can make for a nice mix. It's intellectually stimulating. It's comforting to know that your skills and professional network won't go completely dormant. If you stayed home full-time for some months before going back to work, you may feel like you're recovering an important part of yourself that went missing. Yet there's also unhurried time with baby.
- Working full-time for pay (whether by choice or not) and trying to balance family life can be a guilt-inducing challenge.

I have done all of the above so far.

To moms or dads staying at home full-time: Yes, we are blessed to get this precious time with our kids. We are also the first generation to think it's normal to parent alone. It's not normal. Please arrange regular child care "just" for a break during the day (see page 134).

To new parents working full-time: If this doesn't feel good to you, and you have the choice, speak out for a flexible or part-time work schedule. That can be scary. But it's on you to set your boundaries. Companies always take as much time as you give them.

To parents satisfied with their work situation: High five! You figured out what works for your family. (Now please share your secrets with the rest of us—zerotofivebook on Facebook.)

Just heading back to work?

If your leave is ending much sooner than you'd like, I'm so sorry. The truth is that US society is not set up to support new families in the critical first year. Instead of feeling guilt that you struggle to manage it all, may I suggest anger at the system (and perhaps, eventually, a passion to change it)? Either way:

Figure out what you can let go of. For dinner, can you pour a jar of sauce over pre-cut stir-fry veggies and call it good? Can you get housecleaning help?

Create a transition between work and home. Maybe you leave five minutes early so you can sit in your car listening to music. Maybe you make a pact not to talk about work until baby goes to bed, so the focus can be on family.

If you wanted to work part-time or less, could you afford it?

Families who get by on less money are not necessarily "lucky." They're making sacrifices (whether voluntarily or, in the case of a job loss, not).

If you plan to live on less than two incomes, it helps to have saved money before baby arrives: an emergency fund, at the very least; maybe a babysitting fund; a paid-off mortgage if you really planned ahead. The main requirement, though, is a commitment to being frugal. Which actually can be rather nice.

Cooking meals from scratch is generally tastier, healthier, and an entertaining way to pass time with a toddler. Buying used instead of new means you won't be upset when baby's jacket gets permanently stained within twenty-four hours, or that toy goes missing, or your own clothes get peed on, or an item is never used at all. Washing cloth diapers and wipes turns out not to be that big a deal. Turning nights out on the town into potlucks and game nights, you find that you connect more deeply with your friends. Driving less, you connect more with your neighborhood. Even trading on the future, like not buying that house right now, quickly feels worth it.

With deliberate planning, I can report, living on less works pretty well.

TRY THIS

Mindfulness is the most important thing you can commit to as a working parent. At work, be at work. At home, be at home. Being truly present, research shows, is a direct path to gratitude and happiness in your life.

What does being present feel like?

Here's an experiment. Try holding your baby but paying more attention to your cell phone for two minutes. Then just hold your baby and feel her skin for two minutes. Then have someone watch baby and go elsewhere to check your phone for two minutes. Notice the difference in how each feels.

Be more, do less

The little moments—the ones where you've chosen to be in the moment, rather than rushing or stressing or looking at your phone—those are the ones that you and your kids will cherish most.

Have you ever vacationed on an island and noticed on the first day that you were walking too fast?

It takes some time, but soon you relax into the pace of your new surroundings. You begin to tuck away your digital distractions, because they don't fit in. You start to smile at strangers who pass by, because they're smiling at you. Your strut slows to a saunter, and your words become drawn out. You let the day unfurl. Maybe you sit down next to the elderly man outside the café and chat for a bit. Maybe you lay down in a grassy park to watch the clouds float by and notice the sun warming your skin. It feels luxurious. It's so unlike a typical hurried and harried weekday at home.

An island vacation: that's what babies offer us, if we let them. Babies slow us down. My toddler and I can go for a walk to the park, five blocks away, and it'll take an hour to get there. She'll walk, hop, run, and twirl. She'll stop to fill her pocket, then mine, with rocks. She'll try to spin the wheels of the recycling bins lining the sidewalk, inspect gnarled tree roots, and watch water flowing into a drain. She'll call out the colors of parked cars, point to airplanes in delight, and shout with glee, "There goes the bus!" She'll laugh for seemingly no reason at all. Her joy at the world is contagious. If I try to shoehorn her into my pre-baby expectations of the speed of life, she's cranky and I'm tense. The more I embrace her pace, the nicer it feels to be together.

Baby invites you to slow down. This book is an appeal to accept that invitation.

In this book I've discussed:

- ways to truly connect with your partner, friends, and baby in the moments that make up a day.
- ways to guide instead of punish when baby tests you, an approach that requires taking the long view.
- the importance of embracing emotions, with empathy.
- ideas for moving, playing, and talking together.
- ideas for getting through the tough times with, I hope, a sense of humor.

The philosophies and practical tips in these pages, research tells us, offer our best chance of raising happy and capable children: ones who are aware of and in control of their thoughts, behavior, and emotions.

Knowing this stuff, though, doesn't make it easier to figure out why your newborn is still crying after an hour of walking, patting, and singing. It won't keep your heart from jumping when baby stumbles and falls. You'll still be baffled if one morning you have to persuade your toddler that, yes, she does want her dirty diaper changed. This book won't make it easier to clean beet juice off your light-colored carpet. Or to have patience when baby throws a fit over wearing pants. Or to get your sex life back. Or to (appear to) stay calm when your child leaves bite marks on someone else's child, lies to your face, or blurts out "I hate you!" for the first time.

Being a parent is hard work, no matter who you are. "Perfect" doesn't exist. Allow yourself many, many mistakes. Remember, this is the first time you've parented a 4-month-old, a 14-month-old, or a 4-year-old. And one bad day isn't going to define your child—or you—forever.

The other truth about parenting is that the tough moments quickly fade, because the good moments are so good. Baby smiles up at you or wraps her tiny fingers around one of yours, and your heart melts. Her round cheeks and tiny toes are eminently kissable. As soon as she's able, she puts your shoes on backward and clomps across the room. She runs to the door when you come home, squealing with happiness. She wants to do everything you do: eat your food, carry your bag, wear your clothes, say what you say, help you with your task. She makes connections between concepts that impress you. She snuggles into your lap on the couch for a story. She says the funniest things, and in the cutest voice. She gives you a kiss, or lays her head on your shoulder. When she sleeps, you've never seen any creature so beautiful.

Sometimes even in the middle of being upset, you can't help but smile at how darn cute your kid is. Just this afternoon I was incredibly frustrated that my toddler refused to stay in bed for a nap, and then she stood up on her bed and announced, "I need to get naked now." Babies are bizarre! Multiple times a day, you get to laugh, play, feel intense love, pride and joy, and be absolutely amazed. You may never feel so loved. It's like no other experience.

Everybody says this, but it's true: you're embarking on such a wondrous journey. I hope this book has given you and your baby a good start. And I hope this isn't the end for us. You can continue on with me by signing up at www.zerotofive.net.

Tracy

tracy@zerotofive.net
www.zerotofive.net

Thank you!

This book would not have been possible without the work, love, and support of so many people. My husband, Luke Timmerman, took our daughter on "all-day daddy" outings when deadlines loomed. They even got stuck at Grandma and Grandpa's house, in Wisconsin, during a storm for six days—very helpful!

Photographer Betty Udesen went above and beyond, traveling with us to Hawaii to shoot the cover (that brilliant blue color is real!). And she spent hours with families to capture the beautiful images found throughout the hardcover version of this book. Editor Miles Wray gave encouragement and thoughtful guidance that greatly improved the text.

Designer Nick Johnson worked with the utmost professionalism in creating a lively and inviting book and website. And he made me laugh.

Pear Press publisher Mark Pearson had two excellent ideas: let's publish this book, and let's finish working on it in Hawaii. Marty Westerman asked great questions. Carrie Wicks provided precision proofreading at the speed of light. Publicist Amy Hatch crafted a top-notch plan to get the word out.

Interviews with two parent coaches were invaluable in shaping the guidance section. Sandy Blackard, founder of Language of Listening,® is an incredibly insightful and inspiring parent coach. I feel fortunate to know her and am thrilled to share her work with you. Sarina Natkin has many titles: parent coach, licensed social worker, certified Gottman instructor, certified Positive Discipline trainer, cofounder of Grow Parenting, and fun person to eat cupcakes with.

A big thanks to researchers Adele Diamond, Patricia Kuhl, Megan McClelland, Samuel Mehr, Grover Whitehurst, and Ellen Winner, plus Sandy Blackard and Sarina Natkin, for reviewing specific pages. Thanks to the newbie and veteran parents who rendered opinions of early drafts, including Kris Higginson, Melissa Allison, Ashley Sparks, Luke Timmerman, Kiersten Christensen, Trina Gorman, Nihat Sengul, Marina Cartier, and Carolina Toscano.

A few others knowingly or unknowingly supported this book. Miles and I spent many an hour discussing edits in the café at Metropolitan Market in Lower Queen Anne. Nick and I revised page layouts at Roosters Cafe on Bainbridge Island. Sutra Yoga kept me sane, especially classes by Matthew Coe and Rob and Melissa Lundsgaard. As soon as this book goes off to the printer, Trish Foss will need a spot in this list. I'm ready for a massage.

Thanks so much, everyone, for joining me on this journey.

Will you do me a favor?

I would be so grateful if you took a moment to write a review on Amazon, Goodreads, or your favorite book site. The more reviews a book has, the more visible it will be to others who are searching for help. Your review matters!

If you're not into public displays of affection—or if you have suggestions for improvement—I'd be thrilled to hear from you. **tracy@zerotofive.net**

Age key

Use this age key to jump to pages relevant to your child.

	Page #	Child's age
Prepare		
Peace and quiet, please (at first)	7	0
Bolster your friendships	8	0
Eating for two? Not exactly	10	0
Exercise thirty minutes a day	12	0
Sing or read to your belly	14	0
Stress less	16	0
Share the chores equally	18	0
If you're suffering, get help	22	0
Know you can't truly be prepared	28	0
Envision baby all grown up	30	0
Love		
Prepare to be amazed	34	0, 1
Create a feeling of safety	36	0
Comfort newborn with the familiar	38	0
Cuddle with baby	40	0
Get in sync	42	0, 1, 2
Include baby	45	0, 1, 2, 3

	Page #	Child's age

Talk

Speak in a singsongy voice	50	0, 1
Talk to your baby a ton	52	0, 1, 2, 3
Read together	58	0, 1, 2, 3, 4, 5
Say, "You worked so hard!"	62	1, 2, 3, 4, 5
Teach sign language	68	0, 1
Plan playdates in a second language	71	0, 1, 2, 3, 4, 5

Sleep, eat & potty

Guard your sleep	76	0
Guard baby's sleep, too	78	0
Help baby sleep better at night	80	0
Give baby chances to self-soothe	84	0
Crying it out, a certain way, is OK	88	0, 1
Say "Excuse me" to keep kids in bed	92	3, 4, 5
Make bedtime less crazy	94	3, 4, 5
Be laid-back about breastfeeding	96	0, 1
"Eat food. Not too much. Mostly plants."	98	1, 2, 3, 4, 5
Let baby decide how much to eat	102	1, 2, 3
Offer the opportunity to potty	104	0, 1, 2

	Page #	Child's age

Play

Let baby touch that	108	0, 1, 2
Save the box	109	0, 1, 2, 3, 4, 5
Make music with baby	110	0, 1, 2, 3, 4, 5
When kids snatch toys, wait and see	113	1, 2
Play at self-control	116	3, 4, 5
What makes a great playroom	122	2, 3, 4, 5
Make-believe	124	1, 2, 3, 4, 5
Nurture creativity	128	3, 4, 5
Ask "Why?" and "What if?"	130	3, 4, 5

Connect

Ask for help	134	0, 1, 2, 3, 4, 5
Choose empathy first	136	0, 1, 2, 3, 4, 5
Create more ups than downs	138	0, 1, 2, 3, 4, 5
Know your child	140	0, 1, 2, 3, 4, 5
Hold weekly family meetings	144	3, 4, 5
Put down your phone	146	0, 1, 2, 3, 4, 5
(Almost) no TV before age 2	148	0, 1
A little TV after age 2	150	2, 3, 4, 5
Make screen time social	154	2, 3, 4, 5
Encourage mistakes, discomfort, and boredom	156	1, 2, 3, 4, 5

	Page #	Child's age

Guide

Be firm but warm	160	1, 2, 3, 4, 5
Follow four rules about rules	166	1, 2, 3, 4, 5
Emotion first. Problem second.	170	1, 2, 3, 4, 5
Label intense emotions	172	1, 2, 3, 4, 5
Say what you see	176	1, 2, 3, 4, 5
Guide instead of punish	180	1, 2, 3, 4, 5
Plan ahead to avoid trouble	194	1, 2, 3, 4, 5
Rock your routines	197	0, 1, 2, 3, 4, 5
Call a calm-down, not a time-out	199	3, 4, 5
Ask, "Can you think of a better way?"	202	3, 4, 5

Move

Rock, jiggle, and swing	206	0, 1, 2
Keep moving	208	0, 1, 2, 3, 4, 5

Slow down

Be still	216	0, 1, 2, 3, 4, 5
Don't bother to compare	220	0, 1, 2, 3, 4, 5
Find your own work-family balance	222	0, 1, 2

References

Prepare

Peace and quiet, please (at first)

Petersen, Clarence. "Why Wait for Birth to Begin Talking to Baby?" *Chicago Tribune* 17 Dec. 1987.

"Frequently Asked Questions." *Babyplus: Prenatal Education System*. Web. babyplus.com

De Graaf-Peters, Victorine B., and Mijna Hadders-Algra. "Ontogeny of the Human Central Nervous System: What Is Happening When?" *Early Human Development* 82.4 (2006): 257-66.

Eating for two? Not exactly.

Watkins, Margaret L., Sonja A. Rasmussen, Margaret A. Honein, Lorenzo D. Botto, and Cynthia A. Moore. "Maternal Obesity and Risk for Birth Defects." *Pediatrics* 111.5 (2003): 1152-1158.

Coletta, Jaclyn M., Stacey J. Bell, and Ashley S. Roman. "Omega-3 Fatty Acids and Pregnancy." *Reviews in Obstetrics and Gynecology* 3.4 (2010): 163-71.

Simopoulos, A.P. "The Importance of the Ratio of Omega-6/omega-3 Essential Fatty Acids." *Biomedicine & Pharmacotherapy* 56.8 (2002): 365-79.

Hibbeln, Joseph R., John M. Davis, Colin Steer, Pauline Emmett, Imogen Rogers, Cathy Williams, and Jean Golding. "Maternal Seafood Consumption in Pregnancy and Neurodevelopmental Outcomes in Childhood (ALSPAC Study): An Observational Cohort Study." *The Lancet* 369.9561 (2007): 578-85.

Raatikainen, Kaisa, Nonna Heiskanen, and Seppo Heinonen. "Transition from Overweight to Obesity Worsens Pregnancy Outcome in a BMI-dependent Manner." *Obesity* 14.1 (2006): 165-71.

Scott-Pillai, R., D. Spence, CR Cardwell, A. Hunter, and VA Holmes. "The Impact of Body Mass Index on Maternal and Neonatal Outcomes: A Retrospective Study in a UK Obstetric Population, 2004-2011." *BJOG: An International Journal of Obstetrics and Gynecology* 110.8 (2013): 932-39.

The Endocrine Society. "Pregnant women can prevent excess weight gain with simple steps, study finds." *ScienceDaily*, 6 Jun. 2011.

Exercise 30 minutes a day

Cohn, Meredith. "Hopkins Looks into Fitness Guidelines for Pregnant Women." *The Baltimore Sun* 03 Nov. 2010

Brown, Wendy. "The Benefits of Physical Activity during Pregnancy." *Journal of Science and Medicine in Sport* 5.1 (2002): 37-45.

Melzer, Katarina, Yves Schutz, Michel Boulvain, and Bengt Kayser. "Physical Activity and Pregnancy: Cardiovascular Adaptations, Recommendations and Pregnancy Outcomes." *Sports Medicine* 40.6 (2010): 493-507.

Stress less

Buss, Claudia, Sonja Entringer, James M. Swanson, and Pathik D. Wadhwa. "The Role of Stress in Brain Development: The Gestational Environment's Long-Term Effects on the Brain." *The Dana Foundation*. 25 Apr. 2012. Web. dana.org.

Laplante, David P., Alain Brunet, Norbert Schmitz, Antonio Ciampi, and Suzanne King. "Project Ice Storm: Prenatal Maternal Stress Affects Cognitive and Linguistic Functioning in 5 1/2-Year-Old Children." *Journal of the American Academy of Child and Adolescent Psychiatry* 47.9 (2008): 1063-1072.

"Project Ice Storm: Continuing Effects of Prenatal Stress on Children's Physical, Cognitive, and Behavioural Development in Adolescence." McGill University, 16 July 2012. Web. mcgill.ca.

Sing or read to your belly

Hepper, Peter G., and B. Sara Shahidullah. "Development of Fetal Hearing." *Archives of Disease in Childhood* 71.2 (1994): F81-87.

Babies Listen and Learn While in the Womb (quote from Patricia Kuhl: fetus can't hear dad's voice) Web. webmd.com

Share the chores equally

Parker, Kim, and Wendy Wang. "Roles of Moms and Dads Converge as They Balance Work and Family." *Pew Research Social & Demographic Trends*. 14 Mar. 2013. pewsocialtrends.org.

Mundy, Liza. "The Gay Guide to Wedded Bliss." *The Atlantic.* 22 May 2013. Web. theatlantic.com.

Gager, Constance T., and Scott T. Yabiku. "Who Has the Time? The Relationship Between Household Labor Time and Sexual Frequency." *Journal of Family Issues* 31.2 (2010): 135-63.

Shellenbarger, Sue. "Housework Pays Off Between the Sheets." *The Wall Street Journal.* 21 Oct. 2009. Web. wsj.com.

Seppa, Nathan. "Some Chores Linked to Less Sex." *Science News.* 30 Jan. 2013. sciencenews.org.

Ogolsky, Brian G., and Jill R. Bowers. "A Meta-analytic Review of Relationship Maintenance and Its Correlates." *Journal of Social and Personal Relationships.* 30.3 (2013): 343-67.

If you're suffering, get help

Stone, Katherine. "Depression in Men: A Dad's Story of Male Postpartum Depression." *Post-partum Progress.* 24 Apr. 2012. postpartumprogress.com.

Expect conflict as a couple

The Gottman Institute. Bringing Baby Home Program. *The Gottman Institute.* Web. gottman.com.

Heinicke, Christoph M., Donald Guthrie, and Gloria Ruth. "Marital Adaptation, Divorce, and Parent-infant Development: A Prospective Study." *Infant Mental Health Journal* 18.3 (1997): 282-99.

Love

Prepare to be amazed

Meltzoff, Andrew N. "Born to Learn: What Infants Learn from Watching Us." *The Role of Early Experience in Infant Development.* Skillman, New Jersey: Pediatric Institute Publications, 1999.

Gopnik, Alison. "How Babies Think." *Scientific American* July 2010: 76-81.

What Do Babies Think? Perf. Alison Gopnik. TED Talks, 2011. Video.

Reddy, Sumathi. "Wise Beyond Their Years: What Babies Really Know." *The Wall Street Journal.* 11 Feb. 2013. Web. wsj.com.

National Science Foundation. *Young Babies Prefer Helpers over Hinderers.* Web. research.gov.

Eric Lander at Aspen Ideas 2013 Afternoon of Conversation. Perf. Eric Lander. Aspen Ideas Festival. 1 July 2013. Web. aspenideas.org.

Bryner, Jeanna. "Babies' Brains Churning With Activity." *Livescience.* 11 Aug. 2009. livescience.com.

Create a feeling of safety

Dewar, Gwen. "Stress In Babies: How Parents Keep Babies Calm, Happy, and Emotionally

Healthy." *Parenting Science*. 2013. parent-ingscience.com.

Davies, Patrick T., Melissa L. Sturge-Apple, Dante Ciccetti, and E. Mark Cummings. "The Role of Child Adrenocortical Functioning in Pathways Between Interparental Conflict and Child Maladjustment." *Developmental Psychology* 43.4 (2007): 918-30.

Thompson, Laura A., and Wenda R. Trevathan. "Cortisol Reactivity, Maternal Sensitivity, and Learning In Three-Month-Old Infants." *Infant Behavior and Development* 31.1 (2008): 92-106.

McCoy, Kathleen, E. Mark Cummings, and Patrick T. Davies. "Constructive and Destructive Marital Conflict, Emotional Security and Children's Prosocial Behavior." *Journal of Child Psychology and Psychiatry* 50.3 (2009): 270-79.

Graham, Alice M., Philip A. Fisher, and Jennifer H. Pfeifer. "What Sleeping Babies Hear: An FMRI Study of Interparental Conflict and Infants' Emotion Processing." *Psychological Science* 24.5 (2013): 782-89.

Rutter, Michael, and Edmund J. Sonuga-Barke. "X. Conclusions: Overview of Findings from the Era Study, Inferences, and Research Implication." *Monographs of the Society for Research in Child Development* 75.1 (2010): 212-29.

Comfort newborn with the familiar

Varendi, Heili, Kyllike Christensson, Richard H. Porter, and Jan Winberg. "Soothing Effect of Amniotic Fluid Smell in Newborn Infants." *Early Human Development* 51.1 (1998): 47-55.

Cuddle with baby

Feldman, Ruth, Zehava Rosenthal, and Arthur I. Eidelman. "Maternal-Preterm Skin-to-Skin Contact Enhances Child Physiologic Organization and Cognitive Control Across the First 10 Years of Life." *Biological Psychiatry* 75.1 (2014): 56-64.

Get in sync

Serve-and-return interactions wire the brain: Center on the Developing Child, Harvard University, "Key Concepts: Serve and Return"

Matched interactions activate pleasure center in baby's brain: Reddy, Sumathi. "Wise Beyond Their Years: What Babies Really Know." *The Wall Street Journal.* 11 Feb. 2013.

Lag of less than 1 second: Feldman, Ruth, Romi Magori-Cohen, Giora Galili, Magi Singer, and Yoram Louzoun. "Mother and Infant Coordinate Heart Rhythms through Episodes of Interaction Synchrony." *Infant Behavior and Development* 34.4 (2011): 569-77.

Still Face Experiment (video): Dr. Ed Tronick. Perf. Dr. Ed Tronick. UMass Boston, 2009.

Bick, Johanna, and Mary Dozier. "The Effectiveness of an Attachment-based Intervention in Promoting Foster Mothers' Sensitivity toward Foster Infants." *Infant Mental Health Journal* 34.2 (2013).

Talk

Speak in a singsongy voice

Widdicombe, Lizzie. "Protect & Serve: Partners." *The New Yorker* 8 Oct. 2012: 38-40.

Talk to your baby a ton

University of Washington. News and Information. *While in Womb, Babies Begin Learning Language from Their Mothers. University of Washington.* 2 Jan. 2013. Web. washington.edu.

Stanford University. Stanford Report. *Talking Directly to Toddlers Strengthens Their Language Skills, Stanford Research Shows. Stanford.* 15 Oct. 2013. Web. stanford.edu.

LENA Research Foundation. *Get Accurate Information on Your Child's Language Development with LENA. LENA: Every Word Counts.* Web. lenababy.com.

Moon, Christine, Hugo Lagercrantz, and Patricia K. Kuhl. "Language Experienced in Utero Affects Vowel Perception after Birth: A Two-country Study." *Acta Paediatrica* 102.2 (2013): 156-60. http://ilabs.uw.edu/sites/default/files/2012%20Moon%20et%20al.pdf

Yardley, William. "Betty Hart Dies at 85; Studied Disparities in Children's Vocabulary Growth." *New York Times* 25 Oct. 2012.

Read together

Wasik, Barbara A., and Mary Alice Bond. "Beyond the Pages of a Book: Interactive Book Reading and Language Development in Preschool Classrooms." *Journal of Educational Psychology* 93.2 (2001): 243-50.

Institute of Education Sciences. What Works Clearinghouse. Dialogic Reading. *What Works Clearinghouse.* Institute of Education Sciences, 8 Feb. 2007. Web. ies.ed.gov.

Zuckerman, Barry. "Promoting Early Literacy in Pediatric Practice: Twenty Years of Reach Out and Read." *Pediatrics* 124.6 (2009): 1660-1665.

Reading Rockets. *Dialogic Reading: An Effective Way to Read to Preschoolers. Reading Rockets.* WETA Public Broadcasting. Web. readingrockets.org.

"Dialogic Reading: How to Actively Involve Your Child in Reading." *Reach Out and Read.* Web. reachoutandread.org.

National Institutes of Health. NICHD Publications. *Findings and Determinations of the National Reading Panel by Topic Areas. Eunice Kennedy Shriver National Institute of Child Health and Human Development.* 31 Aug. 2006. Web. nichd.nih.gov.

Blevins, Wiley. "Teach With Phonics Skills Chart." *Scholastic.* Web. scholastic.com.

Cunningham, Anne E., and Keith E. Stanovich. "What Reading Does for the Mind." *Journal of Direct Instruction* 1.2 (2001): 137-49.

Kuo, Alice A., Todd M. Franke, Michael Regalado, and Neal Halfon. "Parent Report of Reading to Young Children." *Pediatrics* 113 (2004): 1944-1951.

Miller, Carolyn, Kathryn Zickuhr, Lee Rainie, and Kristen Purcell. "Parents, Children, Libraries, and Reading – Part 3: Parents and Reading to Children." *Pew Internet.* Pew Research Center, 1 May 2013. Web. libraries.pewinternet.org.

Say, 'You worked so hard!'

Mueller, Claudia M., and Carol S. Dweck. "Praise for Intelligence Can Undermine Children's Motivation and Performance." *Journal of Personality and Social Psychology* 75.1 (1998): 33-52.

Donald, Brooke. "Babies Whose Efforts Are Praised Become More Motivated Kids, Say Stanford Researchers." *Stanford News.* 12 Feb. 2013. Web. news.stanford.edu.

Mueller, C.M., & Dweck, C.S. (1996, April). Implicit theories of intelligence: Relation of parental beliefs to children's expectations. Postersession presented at Head Start's Third National Research Conference, Washington, DC

"You Can Grow Your Intelligence" *Mindset Works.* Web. mindsetworks.com.

Dweck, Carol S. "Brainology: Transforming Students' Motivation to Learn." *Independent School Magazine* Winter 2008. Web. nais.org.

Teach sign language

Thompson, Rachel H., Nicole M. Cotnoir-Bichelman, and Kelly A. Dancho. "Enhancing Early Communication through Infant Sign Training." *Journal of Applied Behavior Analysis* 40.1 (2007): 15-23.

Thompson, Rachel H., Paige M. McKerchar, and Kelly A. Dancho. "The Effects of Delayed Physical Prompts and Reinforcement on Infant Sign Language Acquisition." *Journal of Applied Behavior Analysis* 37.3 (2004): 379-83.

Normand, Matthew P., Mychal A. Machado, and Allison J. Morley. "Infant Sign Training and Functional Analysis." *Journal of Applied Behavior Analysis* 44.2 (2011): 305-14.

Barnes, Susan Kubic. "Sign Language With Babies: What Difference Does It Make?" *Dimensions of Early Childhood* 38.1 (2010): 21-30.

Daniels, Marilyn. "Happy Hands: The Effect of ASL on Hearing Children's Literacy." *Reading Research and Instruction* 44.1 (2004): 86-100.

Mohler, James L. *The Visual-Spatial System.* Purdue University. PDF.

Plan playdates in a second language

Kuhl, Patricia K. "Early Language Learning and Literacy: Neuroscience Implications for Education." *Mind, Brain, and Education* 5.3 (2011): 128-42.

Kuhl, Patricia K., Feng-Ming Tsao, and Huei-Mei Liu. "Foreign-language Experience in Infancy: Effects of Short-term Exposure and Social Interaction on Phonetic Learning." *Proceedings of the National Academy of Sciences of the United States of America* 100.15 (2003): 9096-9101.

Bhattacharjee, Yudhijit. "Why Bilinguals Are Smarter." *New York Times.* 17 Mar. 2012. Web. nytimes.com.

The Linguistic Genius of Babies. Patricia Kuhl. *TEDxRainier.* TED Talks, Feb. 2011. Web. ted.com.

Grosjean, François. "What Parents Want to Know about Bilingualism." *The Bilingual Family Newsletter* 26.4 (2009): 1-6. *François Grosjean: Professor Emeritus.* Web. francois-grosjean.ch.

Meade, Stephanie. "Why OPOL Doesn't Always Work." *InCulture Parent: For Parents Raising Little Global Citizens.* N.p., 24 Apr. 2013. Web. incultureparent.com.

"From Linguist to Mum: Looking Back." *The Piri-Piri Lexicon.* 23 Apr. 2013. Web. thepiripirilexicon.com.

Sleep, Eat, and Potty

Guard your sleep

Callahan, Alice. "Why Sleep Matters to Babies and Parents." *Science of Mom: The Heart and Science of Parenting.* 13 Feb. 2012. Web. scienceofmom.com.

"Changes in Sleep with Age." *Healthy Sleep.* Division of Sleep Medicine at Harvard Medical School, 18 Dec. 2007. Web. healthysleep.med.harvard.edu.

McKenna, James J. "Cosleeping and Biological Imperatives: Why Human Babies Do Not and Should Not Sleep Alone." *Neuroantrhopology.* 21 Dec. 2008. Web. neuroanthropology.net.

Mindell, Jodi A., Lorena S. Telofski, Benjamin Wiegand, and Ellen S. Kurtz. "A Nightly Bedtime Routine: Impact on Sleep in Young Children and Maternal Mood." *Sleep.* 32.5 (2009): 599-606.

Help baby sleep better at night

Skuladottir, A., and M. Thome. "Changes in Infant Sleep Problems after a Family-centered Intervention." *Pediatric Nursing* 29.5 (2003): 375-78.

McKenna, James J. "Cosleeping and Biological Imperatives: Why Human Babies Do Not and Should Not Sleep Alone." *Neuroantrhopology.* 21 Dec. 2008. Web. neuroanthropology.net.

Dewar, Gwen. "Bed sharing with infants: Can it be done safely?" *Parenting Science.* parentingscience.com.

Gerard, Claudia M., Kathleen A. Harris, and Bradley T. Thach. "Spontaneous Arousals in Supine Infants While Swaddled and Unswaddled During Rapid Eye Movement and Quiet Sleep." *Pediatrics* 110.6 (2002).

Mindell, Jodi A., Lorena S. Telofski, Benjamin Wiegand, and Ellen S. Kurtz. "A Nightly Bedtime Routine: Impact on Sleep in Young Children and Maternal Mood." *Sleep.* 32.5 (2009): 599-606.

Crying it out, a certain way, is OK

Price, Anna M.H., Melissa Wake, Obioha C. Ukoumunne, and Harriet Hiscock. "Five-Year Follow-up of Harms and Benefits of Behavioral Infant Sleep Intervention: Randomized Trial." *Pediatrics.* 9 Sept. 2012. Web.

Ferber, Richard. Solve Your Child's Sleep Problems: *The World's Bestselling Guide to Helping Your Child Sleep through the Night.* London: Vermilion, 2013.

Weissbluth, Marc. *Healthy Sleep Habits, Happy Child: A Step-by-step Program for a Good Night's Sleep.* New York: Ballantine, 2005.

Make bedtime less crazy

Benaroya, Melissa. "Is It Time For Your Family To Hit The Charts? (And We Are Not Talkin' Top 40)." *Grow Parenting: Cultivating Healthy Families.* 5 Mar. 2013. Web. growparenting.com.

Nelson, Jane, and Katie Clark. "Routines." *Positive Discipline.* 19 Oct. 2010. Web. positivediscipline.com.

Natkin, Sarina Behar. "Crazy Time: A Solution For Bedtimes Gone Wild." *Grow Parenting: Cultivating Healthy Families.* 8 June 2011. Web. growparenting.com

Be laid-back about breastfeeding

Shute, Nancy. "To Succeed At Breast-Feeding, Most New Moms Could Use Help." *NPR.* 23 Sept. 2013.

Underwood, Tripp. "Can Breastfeeding for Longer Make a Child Smarter?" *Thriving – Child's Hospital Boston's Pediatric Health Blog.* 31 July 2013. childrenshospitalblog.org.

'Eat food. Not too much. Mostly plants.'

Moss, Michael. "The Extraordinary Science of Addictive Junk Food." *New York Times.* 20 Feb. 2013.

Satter, Ellyn. "Eating Competence: Definition and Evidence for the Satter Eating Competence Model." *Journal of Nutrition Education and Behavior* 39.5 (2007): S142-153.

Wardle, J., M-L Herrera, L. Cooke, and E.L. Gibson. "Modifying Children's Food Preferences: The Effects of Exposure and Reward on Acceptance of an Unfamiliar Vegetable." *European Journal of Clinical Nutrition* 57 (2003): 341-348.

Blissett, Jacqueline, Carmel Bennett, Jessica Donohoe, Samantha Rogers, and Suzanne Higgs. "Predicting Successful Introduction of Novel Fruit to Preschool Children." *Journal of the Academy of Nutrition and Dietetics* 112.12 (2012): 1959-1967.

Vollrath, Margarete E., Serena Tonstad, Mary K. Rothbart, and Sarah E. Hampson. "Infant Temperament Is Associated with Potentially Obesogenic Diet at 18 Months." *International Journal of Pediatric Obesity* 6.2 (2011): 408-14.

"Farmers' Market Tips: Storing Fruits & Vegetables." *Ecology Center.* Web. ecologycenter.org.

Let baby decide how much to eat

Satter, Ellyn. "Eating Competence: Definition and Evidence for the Satter Eating Competence Model." *Journal of Nutrition Education and Behavior* 39.5 (2007): S142-153.

Offer the opportunity to potty

Dewar, Gwen. "Infant toilet training: An evidence-based guide." *Parenting Science.* parentingscience.com.

Dewar, Gwen. "The science of toilet training: What research tells us about timing." *Parenting Science.* parentingscience.com.

Dewar, Gwen. "Toilet training in less than a day? An evidence-based review of 'fast-track' toilet training techniques." *Parenting Science.* parentingscience.com.

Moyer, Melinda Wenner. "Slate's Definitive Guide to Potty Training." *Slate*. 8 July 2013. Web. slate.com.

Shute, Nancy. "Why Toilet Training Can Trip Up Parents and Doctors." *National Public Radio*. 8 Aug. 2011. Web. npr.org.

Play

When kids snatch toys, wait and see

Svetlova, Margarita, Sara R. Nichols, and Celia A. Brownell. "Toddlers' Prosocial Behavior: From Instrumental to Empathic to Altruistic Helping." *Child development* 81.6 (2010): 1814–1827. PMC. Web. 5 Dec. 2014.

Make music with baby

Gerry, David, Andrea Unrau, and Laurel J. Trainor. "Active Music Classes in Infancy Enhance Musical, Communicative and Social Development." *Developmental Science* 15.3 (2012): 398-407.

Hull, Kathryn B. "Why Teach Music?" *Music Teachers of the Desert*. California Association of Professional Music Teachers, 1999. Web. mtod.us.

Mehr, Samuel A., Adena Schachner, Rachel C. Katz, and Elizabeth S. Spelke. "Two Randomized Trials Provide No Consistent Evidence for Nonmusical Cognitive Benefits of Brief Preschool Music Enrichment." *PLoS ONE* 8.12 (2007).

Play at self-control

Diamond, Adele, and Kathleen Lee. "Interventions Shown to Aid Executive Function Development in Children 4–12 Years Old." *Science* 333.6045 (2011): 959-64.

Tominey, Shauna L., and Megan M. McClelland. "Red Light, Purple Light: Findings From a Randomized Trial Using Circle Time Games to Improve Behavioral Self-Regulation in Pre-school." *Early Education and Development* 22.3 (2011): 489-519.

Wanless, SB, MM McClelland, AC Acock, CC Ponitz, SH Son, X. Lan, FJ Morrison, JL Chen, FM Chen, K. Lee, M. Sung, and S. Li. "Measuring Behavioral Regulation in Four Societies." *Psychological Assessment* 23.2 (2011): 364-78.

Valiente, Carlos, Nancy Eisenberg, Rg Haugen, Tracy L. Spinrad, Claire Hofer, Jeffrey Liew, and Anne Kupfer. "Children's Effortful Control and Academic Achievement: Mediation Through Social Functioning." *Early Education and Development* 22.3 (2011): 411-33.

"Preschool Children Who Can Pay Attention More Likely to Finish College: Early Reading and Math Not Predictive of College Completion." *Science Daily*. 6 Aug. 2012. Web. sciencedaily.com.

Shute, Nancy. "For Kids, Self-Control Factors Into Future Success." *National Public Radio*. 11 Feb. 2011. Web. npr.org.

Bernier, Annie, Stephenie M. Carlson, and Natasha Whipple. "From External Regulation to Self-Regulation: Early Parenting Precursors of Young Children's Executive Functioning." *Child Development* 81.1 (2010): 326-39.

Aamodt, Sandra. "How Self-Control Develops." *Big Think*. N.p., 25 Mar. 2012. Web. bigthink.com.

Aamodt, Sandra, and Sam Wang. "Building Self-Control, the American Way." *New York Times*. 17 Feb. 2012. Web. nytimes.com.

Blair, Clancy, and Rachel Peters Razza. "Relating Effortful Control, Executive Function, and False Belief Understanding to Emerging Math and Literacy Ability in Kindergarten." *Child Development* 78.2 (2007): 647-63.

Bull, Rebecca, and Gala Scerif. "Executive Functioning as a Predictor of Children's Mathematics Ability: Inhibition, Switching, and Working Memory." *Developmental Neuropsychology* 19.3 (2001): 273-93.

Gathercole, Susan E., Claire Tiffany, Josie Briscoe, and Annabel Thorn. "Developmental Consequences of Poor Phonological Short-term Memory Function in Childhood: A Longitudinal Study." *Journal of Child Psychology and Psychiatry* 46.6 (2005): 598-611.

What a great playroom looks like

Medina, John. "Brain Rules for Baby." Pear Press, 2010.

Make-believe

Diamond, Adele, W. Steven Barnett, Jessica Thomas, and Sarah Munro. "Preschool Program Improves Cognitive Control." *Science* 318.5855 (2007): 1387-388.

Willingham, Daniel. "Tools of the Mind: Promising Pre-k Curriculum Looking Less Promising." 27 Aug. 2012. Web. danielwillingham.com.

Paul, Annie Murphy. "In The Brilliant Report: Studies On Executive Function And Exercise." 11 Mar. 2013. Web. anniemurphypaul.com.

Nurture creativity

Shaughnessy, Michael F. "An Interview with E. Paul Torrance: About Creativity."*Educational Psychology Review* 10.4 (1998): 441-52.

Azzam, Amy M. "Why Creativity Now? A Conversation with Sir Ken Robinson."*Educational Leadership* 67.1 (2009): 22-26.

Ogletree, Earl J. "The Comparative Status of the Creative Thinking Ability of Waldorf Education Students: A Survey." Sept. 1996. Web. thebee.se.

Ask 'Why?' and 'What if?'

Dyer, Jeffrey H., Hal B. Gregerson, and Clayton M. Christensen. "The Innovator's DNA." *Harvard Business Review.* Dec. 2009. hbr.org.

Dyer, Jeff, and Hal Gregerson. "Learn How to Think Different(ly)." *Harvard Business Review Blog Network.* 27 Sept. 2011. Web. blogs.hbr.org.

Dyer, Jeffrey H., Hal B. Gregersen, and Clayton Christensen. "Entrepreneur Behaviors, Opportunity Recognition, and the Origins of Innovative Ventures." *Strategic Entrepreneurship Journal* 2.4 (2008): 317-38.

"Avoiding Ivy League Preschool Syndrome." *Mr. Money Mustache.* 12 Oct. 2011. Web. mrmoneymustache.com.

5 Dangerous Things You Should Let Your Kids Do. Perf. Gerver Tulley. *TED Talks.* Mar. 2007. Web. ted.com.

Connect

Choose empathy first

The Gottman Institute. *Research FAQs.* Web. gottman.com.

Create more ups than downs

Gottman, John, and Nan Silver. "What Makes Marriage Work?" *Psychology Today.* 1 Mar. 1994. Web. psychologytoday.com.

The Gottman Institute. *Research FAQs.* Web. gottman.com.

Know your child

Van Den Boom, Dymphna C. "The Influence of Temperament and Mothering on Attachment and Exploration: An Experimental Manipulation of Sensitive Responsiveness among Lower-Class Mothers with Irritable Infants." *Child Development* 65.5 (1994): 1457-477.

Ollendick, Thomas H., and Ronald J. Prinz, eds. *Advances in Clinical Psychology.* Vol. 19. New York City: Plenum, 1977.

McClowery, Sandra Graham, Eileen T. Rodriguez, and Robyn Koslowitz. "Temperament-Based Intervention: Re-examining Goodness of Fit." *European Journal of Developmental Science* 2.1 (2008): 120-35.

"Tips on Temperament." *Zero to Three: National Center for Infants, Toddlers, and Families.* Web. zerotothree.org.

Hold weekly family meetings

Feiler, Bruce S. *The Secrets of Happy Families: Improve Your Mornings, Rethink Family Dinner, Fight Smarter, Go out and Play, and Much More.* New York, NY: William Morrow, 2013.

Put down your phone

Boone, R. Thomas, and Joseph G. Cunningham. "Children's Decoding of Emotion in Expressive Body Movement: The Development of Cue Attunement." *Developmental Psychology* 34 (1998): 1007-016.

Liebal, Kristin, Malinda Carpenter, and Michael Tomasello. "Young Children's Understanding of Markedness in Non-verbal Communication." *Journal of Child Language* 38.4 (2011): 888-903.

(Almost) no TV before age 2

"Media Use by Children Younger Than 2 Years." *Pediatrics* 128.5 (2011): 1040-1045.

Zimmerman, Frederick K., Dimitri A. Christakis, and Andrew N. Meltzoff. "Television and DVD/Video Viewing in Children Younger Than 2 Years." *Archives of Pediatrics & Adolescent Medicine* 161.5 (2007): 473-79.

A little TV after age 2

"Council on Communications and Media: Children, Adolescents, and the Media." *Pediatrics* (2013). 28 Oct. 2013. Web.

Linebarger, Deborah L., and Dale Walker. "Infants' and Toddlers' Television Viewing and Language Outcomes." *American Behavioral Scientist* 48.5 (2005): 624-45.

Saint Louis, Catherine. "Certain Television Fare Can Help Ease Aggression in Young Children, Study Finds." *New York Times.* 18 Feb. 2013. Web. nytimes.com.

Shaw, Jonathan. "The Deadliest Sin." *Harvard Business Review.* Mar.-Apr. 2004. Web. hbr.org.

Rideout, Victoria, and Elizabeth Hamel. "The Media Family: Electronic Media in the Lives of Infants, Toddlers, Preschoolers, and Their Parents." *Kaiser Family Foundation.* May 2006. Web. kaiserfamilyfoundation.files.wordpress.com.

Parker-Pope, Tara. "TV Background Noise Disrupts Child Play." *New York Times.* 16 July 2008. Web. nytimes.com.

Schmidt, Marie Evans, Tiffany A. Pempek, Heather L. Kirkorian, Anne Frankenfield Lund, and Daniel R. Anderson. "The Effects of Background Television on the Toy Play Behavior of Very Young Children." *Child Development* 79.4 (2008): 1137-1151.

Ostrov, Jaime M., Douglas A. Gentile, and Adam D. Mullins. "Evaluating the Effect of Educational Media Exposure on Aggression in Early Childhood." *Journal of Applied Developmental Psychology* 34 (2012): 38-44.

Mendelsohn, A.L., C.A. Brockmeyer, B.P. Dreyer, A.H. Fierman, S. Berkule-Silberman, and S. Tomopoulos. "Do Verbal Interactions with Infants during Electronic Media Exposure Mitigate Adverse Impacts on Their Language Development as Toddlers?" *Infant and Child Development* 19 (2010): 577-93.

Mares, M.L., and E. Acosta. "Be Kind to Three-legged Dogs: Children's Literal Interpretations of TV's Moral Lessons." *Media Psychology* 11.3 (2008): 377-99.

"Television and the Under 3 Crowd: Making Good Decisions About "Screen Time" for Young Children." *Zero to Three: National Center for Infants, Toddlers, and Families.* 2009. Web. zerotothree.org.

Tandon, PS, C. Zhou, P. Lozano, and DA Christakis. "Preschoolers' Total Daily Screen Time at Home and by Type of Child Care." *Journal of Pediatrics* 158.2 (2011): 297-300.

Dennison, Barbara A., Theresa J. Russo, Patrick A. Burdick, and Paul L. Jenkins. "An Intervention to Reduce Television Viewing by Preschool Children." *Archives of Pediatrics & Adolescent Medicine* 158.2 (2004): 170-76.

Make screen time social

Worthen, Ben. "What Happens When Toddlers Zone Out With an IPad." *The Wall Street Journal*. 22 May 2012. Web. wsj.com.

Hu, Elise. "What You Need To Know About Babies, Toddlers And Screen Time."*National Public Radio*. 28 Oct. 2013. Web. npr.org.

"Council on Communications and Media: Children, Adolescents, and the Media."*Pediatrics* (2013). 28 Oct. 2013. Web.

Semeniuk, Ivan. "The murky distinction between educational and 'mindless' screen time." *The Globe and Mail*. N.p., 30 Aug. 2013. Web. theglobeandmail.com.

Almond, Steve. "My Kids Are Obsessed With Technology, and It's All My Fault." *New York Times*. 21 June 2013. Web. nytimes.com.

Shapiro, Jordan. "Why Playing Video Games Makes You a Better Dad." *Forbes*. 15 Nov. 2012. Web. forbes.com.

Degnan, Taryn. "How Touchscreens Are Changing the World for Kids." *Common Sense Media*. 9 May 2013. Web. commonsensemedia.org.

Shute, Nancy. "Kids Watch TV As Parents Do, Not As They Say." *National Public Radio*. 15 July 2013. Web. npr.org.

Painter, Kim. "Most Parents Not Worried about Children's Screen Time." *USA Today*. 4 June 2013. Web. usatoday.com.

"Parents' TV Viewing Habits Influence Kids' Screen Time." *American Academy of Pediatrics*. 15 July 2013. Web. aap.org.

Neyfakh, Leon. "Why You Can't Stop Checking Your Phone." *The Boston Globe*. 6 Oct. 2013. Web. bostonglobe.com.

Encourage mistakes, discomfort, and boredom

Carey, Benedict. "You're Bored, but Your Brain Is Tuned In." *New York Times*. 5 Aug. 2008. Web. nytimes.com.

Guide

Be firm but warm

Maccoby, Eleanor E. "Parenting and Its Effects on Children: On Reading and Misreading Behavior Genetics." *Annual Review of Psychology* 51 (2000): 1-27.

Dewar, Gwen. "Permissive parenting: A parenting science guide to the research." *Parenting Science*. parentingscience.com.

Baumrind, Diana. "The Influence of Parenting Style of Adolescent Competence and Substance Use." *The Journal of Early Adolescence* 11.1 (1991): 56-95.

Follow four rules about rules

Medina, John. "Brain Rules for Baby." Pear Press, 2010.

Label intense emotions

Herbert, Cornelia, Anca Sfärlea, and Terry Blumenthal. "Your Emotion or Mine: Labeling Feelings Alters Emotional Face Perception—an ERP Study on Automatic and Intentional Affect Labeling." *Frontiers in Human Neuroscience* 7 (2013).

"Putting Feelings Into Words Produces Therapeutic Effects In The Brain." *Science Daily*. 22 June 2007. Web. sciencedaily.com.

Denham, S.A., and R. Burton. "A Social-emotional Intervention for At-risk 4-year-olds."*Journal of School Psychology* 34.3 (1996): 225-45.

Domitrovich, C.E., R. Cortes, and M.T. Greenberg. "Preschool PATHS: Promoting Social and

Emotional Competence in Young Children." Proc. of 6th National Head Start Research Conference, Washington, D.C.

Moore, B., and K. Beland. "Evaluation of Second Step, Preschool-kindergarten: A Violence Prevention Curriculum Kit." Proc. of Committee for Children, Seattle, Washington.

Webster-Stratton, C., and M. Hammond. "Treating Children with Early-onset Conduct Problems: A Comparison of Child and Parent Training Interventions." *Journal of Consulting and Clinical Psychology* 65.1 (1997): 93-109.

Say what you see

Blackard, Sandra R. "Say What You See for Parents and Teachers." Author, 2011.

Guide instead of punish

Steinberg, Laurence. "Authoritative Parenting and Adolescent Adjustment Across Varied Ecological Niches." Presented at the Biennial Meeting of the Society for Research in Child Development (Kansas City, MO, April 1989). http://eric.ed.gov/?id=ED324558

Tangney, JP, P. Wagner, C. Fletcher, and R. Gramzow. "Shamed into Anger? The Relation of Shame and Guilt to Anger and Self-reported Aggression." *Journal of Personality and Social Psychology* 62.4 (1992): 669-75.

Natkin, Sarina Behar. "Help! My Preschooler Is Hitting!" *Grow Parenting: Cultivating Healthy Families.* 15 May 2012. Web. growparenting.com.

Bayer, Alicia. "Attachment Parenting 101: What Should I Do If My Child Talks Back?" *Examiner.* 17 Sept. 2010. Web. examiner.com.

"The Discipline of Squats." *Blue Cotton Memory.* 20 July 2009. Web. bluecottonmemory.wordpress.com.

Bronson, Po. "Learning to Lie." *New York Magazine.* 10 Feb. 2008. Web. nymag.com.

"Responding to Misbehavior." *Responsive Classroom.* Nov. 2011. Web. responsiveclassroom.org.

Kohlberg, L. "The Development of Children's Orientations toward a Moral Order." *Vita Humana* 6 (1963): 11-33.

Rock your routines

Feiler, Bruce S. *The Secrets of Happy Families: Improve Your Mornings, Rethink Family Dinner, Fight Smarter, Go out and Play, and Much More.* New York, NY: William Morrow, 2013.

Call a calm-down, not a time-out

Moyer, Melinda Wenner. "Are Timeouts Messing Up Your Kids?" Slate. 24 Apr. 2013. Web. slate.com.

Morawska, Alina, and Matthew Sanders. "Parental Use of Time Out Revisited: A Useful or Harmful Parenting Strategy?" *Journal of Child and Family Studies* 20.1 (2011): 1-8.

Erford, Bradley T. "A Modified Time-out Procedure for Children with Noncompliant or Defiant Behaviors." *Professional School Counseling* 2.3 (1999): 205-10.

Roberts, Mark W., Robert J. McMahon, Rex Forehand, and Lewis Humphreys. "The Effect of Parental Instruction-giving on Child Compliance." *Behavior Therapy* 9.5 (1978): 793-98.

Ask, 'Can you think of a better way?'

Kamins, Melissa L., and Carol S. Dweck. "Person Versus Process Praise and Criticism: Implications for Contingent Self-Worth and Coping." *Developmental Psychology* 35.3 (1999): 835-47.

Move

Rock, jiggle, and swing

Eliot, Lise. *What's Going on in There?: How the Brain and Mind Develop in the First Five Years of Life.* New York, NY: Bantam, 1999.

Keep moving

Shaw, Jonathan. "The Deadliest Sin." *Harvard Business Review*. Mar.-Apr. 2004. Web. hbr.org.

"Exercise: A Changing Perscription." *Harvard Business Review*. Mar.-Apr. 2004. Web. hbr.org.

Vlahos, James. "Is Sitting a Lethal Activity?" *New York Times*. 14 Apr. 2011. Web. nytimes.com.

Ananthaswamy, Anil. "Why Is Exercise Such a Chore?" *Slate*. N.p., 16 June 2013. Web. slate.com.

"Sitting Time Associated with Increased Risk of Chronic Diseases." *Kansas State University News and Editorial Services*. 18 Feb. 2013. Web. k-state.edu.

George, Emma S., Richard R. Rosenkranz, and Gregory S. Kolt. "Chronic Disease and Sitting Time in Middle-aged Australian Males: Findings from the 45 and Up Study." *International Journal of Behavioral Nutrition and Physical Activity* 10.20 (2013).

Dworley. "Fancy Ikea Treadmill Desk." *Instructables*. N.p., n.d. Web. instructables.com.

Slow Down

Be still

Bhanoo, Sindya N. "How Meditation May Change the Brain." *New York Times*. 28 Jan. 2011. Web. nytimes.com.

"Scientific Evidence That Transcendental Meditation Works." *David Lynch Foundation*. Web. davidlynchfoundation.org.

Hölzel, Britta K., James Carmody, Mark Vangel, Christina Congleton, Sita M. Yerramsetti, Tim Gard, and Sara W. Lazar. "Mindfulness Practice Leads to Increases in Regional Brain Gray Matter Density." *Psychiatry Research: Neuroimaging* 191.1 (2011): 36-43.

Hanc, John. "In Sitting Still, a Bench Press for the Brain." *New York Times*. N.p., 9 May 2012. Web. nytimes.com.

Lutz, A., J. Brefczynski-Lewis, T. Johnstone, and RJ Davidson. "Regulation of the Neural Circuitry of Emotion by Compassion Meditation: Effects of Meditative Expertise." *PLoS ONE* 26.3 (2008).

Blakeslee, Sandra. "Study Suggests Meditation Can Help Train Attention." *New York Times*. 8 May 2007. Web. nytimes.com.

Hoffman, Jan. "How Meditation Might Boost Your Test Scores." *New York Times*. 3 Apr. 2013. Web. nytimes.com.

Micucci, Dana. "International Education: Meditation Helps Students." *New York Times*. 15 Feb. 2005. Web. nytimes.com.

"University of Michigan study finds improved emotional development in early adolescent African American children practicing Transcendental Meditation." *David Lynch Foundation*. Web. davidlynchfoundation.org.

Find your own work-family balance

Wang, Wendy. "Mothers and Work: What's 'Ideal'?" *Pew Research Center*. 19 Aug. 2013. Web. pewresearch.org.

Parker, Kim, and Wendy Wang. "Modern Parenthood." *Pew Research Social & Demographic Trends*. 14 Mar. 2013. Web. pewsocialtrends.org.

Buchler, Cheryl, and Marion O'Brien. "Mothers' Part-Time Employment: Associations With Mother and Family Well-Being." *Journal of Family Psychology* 25.6 (2011): 895-906.

Resources

Brain Rules for Baby
by John Medina

Zero to Five is the how, and *Brain Rules for Baby* is the why. It's an engaging read on the best way to raise a smart, happy child through age 5.

Learn more at **www.brainrules.net**

Visit **zerotofive.net** and you'll find:

- **Bonuses just for you.** Get videos, bonus tips, and more at **www.zerotofive. net/bonuses**

- **Bulk orders.** *Zero to Five* is being used by pediatricians, home visitors, childcare providers, early learning advocates, parenting educators, parent support groups, and other professionals. See how: **www.zerotofive. net/connect**

- **Talks & workshops.** You can hire me to speak to your group. See topics at **www.zerotofive.net/speaking**

**Tell a friend! Please let others know about this book
and help spread the positive-parenting movement.**